P9-DXI-989

BOOKS BY THE SAME AUTHORS

Love Is Letting Go of Fear
Teach Only Love
Goodbye to Guilt
Out of the Darkness into the Light
Love Is the Answer: Creating Positive Relationships
To Give Is to Receive:
An 18 Day Mini-Course on Healing Relationships
One Person Can Make a Difference
Wake-Up Calls

AND FOR CHILDREN
Me First and the Gimme Gimmes

AUDIO CASSETTES

Love Is Letting Go of Fear
Teach Only Love
Goodbye to Guilt
Love Is the Answer: Creating Positive Relationships
To Give Is to Receive
Forgiveness Is the Key to Happiness
Introduction to *A Course in Miracles*
One Person Can Make a Difference
The Quiet Mind
Achieving Inner Peace
Visions of the Future I
Finding the Miracle of Love in Your Life:
Based on *A Course in Miracles*

VIDEO CASSETTES

Achieving Inner and Outer Success
Healing Relationships
Visions of the Future I

If you wish information on Jerry Jampolsky's and Diane Cirincione's lecture and workshop schedule, or if you wish to purchase books or audio or video cassette tapes, please send a self addressed envelope to P.O. Box 1012, Tiburon, CA 94920 or call 1-800-359-2246.

CHANGE YOUR MIND, CHANGE YOUR LIFE

CONCEPTS IN ATTITUDINAL HEALING

❖

GERALD G. JAMPOLSKY, M.D.,
and
DIANE V. CIRINCIONE

MJF BOOKS
NEW YORK

Published by MJF Books
Fine Communications
Two Lincoln Square
60 West 66th Street
New York, NY 10023

Change Your Mind, Change Your Life
LC Control Number 2001012345
ISBN 1-56731-514-3

Copyright © 1993 by Gerald G. Jampolsky, M.D. and Diane V. Cirincione

This edition published by arrangement with Bantam Books, an imprint of the Bantam Dell Publishing Group, a division of Random House, Inc.

Portions from *A Course in Miracles* © 1975. Reprinted by permission of the Foundation for Inner Peace, Inc., P.O. Box 1104, Glen Ellen, California 95442. *A Course in Miracles* may be purchased from the Foundation for Inner Peace. The three-volume hardcover set is $40. The single volume (all in one) softcover is $25. The hardcover (all in one) is $30.

All rights reserved. No part of this publication may be reproduced or transmitted in any form or by any means, electronic or mechanical, including photocopy, recording, or any information storage and retrieval system, without the prior written permission of the publisher.

Manufactured in the United States of America on acid-free paper
MJF Books and the MJF colophon are trademarks of Fine Creative Media, Inc.

BG   10 9 8 7 6 5 4 3 2 1

We dedicate this book with boundless gratitude and love to the many children and adults who have come to our center to seek help and who have become our teachers, to the many volunteers who have contributed so much, and to the uniquely committed staff at the Center for Attitudinal Healing in Tiburon, California.

ACKNOWLEDGMENTS

We wish to express our deepest gratitude and appreciation to Hal Zina Bennett, not only for the many helpful hours he spent editing this book but also for his part in making it such a joyful process. We treasure his friendship with us.

We also wish to acknowledge Tom Ingstad and Debbie Ward Ingstad for their Hawaiian hospitality and for giving us the opportunity to write much of this book in such a beautiful environment.

We are most thankful for the wonderful support and encouragement of our dear friend Michelle Rapkin, who has been our editor at Bantam Books.

We wish to acknowledge that the foundation for this book is based on principles from *A Course in Miracles,* and we are most grateful to Judith Skutch Whitson and Robert Skutch, of the Foundation for Inner Peace, for their permission to quote from the Course. References for the quotations, which we have borrowed from the Course, can be found in the notes section at the back of the book.

CONTENTS

Part III
Attitudinal Healing—
Eighteen Weekly Lessons

*Whether we live our lives
filled with peace or conflict
is ultimately determined by our attitudes.*

PREFACE

Most of us want to be at peace in our lives. But it seems as if circumstances are always intruding to make that impossible. If you are like us, even opening up the newspaper in the morning and reading about war and bloodshed taking place throughout the world can make any peace of mind you might have thought you had quickly disappear.

We can be faced with a host of things that happen before we even leave our homes in the morning that we can blame for our lack of peace. We can have a disagreement with our partner over how to handle a problem that has come up with one of our children, and this can leave us feeling angry and out of sorts. Or maybe we discover that someone in our household failed to give us an important telephone message, and we feel that they are to blame for the upset we are feeling.

Our car won't start because the battery is dead, and this can cause our whole day to be ruined. Or the neighbor calls to say he is going to sue us because our tree has caused damage to his roof. We open up an envelope and find a bill from the doctor that we think is outrageously high and unjustified. We feel ripped off, and when we feel this way, it is easy for us to believe that there's a real enemy out there and that we are victims. It is difficult, indeed, to believe that we could possibly have a choice about the ideas and feelings we hold in our minds.

We get to the office and find out that the computer program we just purchased isn't doing the job we were promised it would. Our boss calls us into her office and bawls us out because we didn't stick to our budget.

Or maybe our family physician calls to advise us that our elderly mother needs to be placed in a rest home where her medication can be supervised, yet we know how much she wants to stay in her own home.

Or you are an older person and you feel rejected and alone because your children never seem to phone or visit you.

Truly the list of things that we are capable of getting upset about seems endless. However, the ideas presented in this book are based on the premise that we can change the angry, fearful, negative thoughts in our minds. We need not be victims of events occurring in the world around us. Each instant provides us with a new opportunity to reexamine our lives and to choose, once again, what it is we want to experience—love or fear, peace or conflict.

The Principles of Attitudinal Healing, from which these ideas are drawn, teach us that happiness is our natural state and that we can choose to have peace of mind as our only goal.

To change our lives, we need only change our minds. Instead of holding on to grievances, blaming others, or condemning ourselves, we can *choose to have a willingness* to forgive, to let go of all such thoughts. Through that willingness to forgive we take an important step toward correcting our misperceptions and removing the obstacles to our experience of happiness and peace.

Of course in nearly everything we do—at home, work, or school; while sitting in the doctor's office; at the shopping mall; or perhaps while trying to get information at a government office—we are involved in relationships with other people. And in each of these activities there is always the potential for conflict, anger, and resentment.

Without thinking about it we often set up rules for communication with our loved ones that are entirely different from the rules we follow with the people outside our immediate families. It may be easy to forgive your child or partner, but you may not be as willing to forgive people with whom you work.

If you are a parent, you may get upset because you feel your child's teacher doesn't like him or her. Or, if you are a teacher or principal, you may be distressed because you think that many parents are neglecting their children.

Whether you are a physician, dentist, lawyer, or other professional offering your services, or a person who is the recipient of them, there is always the temptation to blame the other person for causing you to feel pressured and upset, as if that person had the power to take away your peace of mind.

Wherever we go and whatever we do, there always seems to be the temptation to judge or condemn others and to find others to blame for what we are feeling. Furthermore we have all had past experiences that seem to "prove" to us that we must be careful about whom we trust. We find ourselves filled with doubts and fearful that others will take advantage of us.

A DIFFERENT PATH

Is there another way of looking at the world? Are there other ways for communicating with each other? Is it possible to change the belief that to survive in the world and not be a victim we must constantly be ready to defend and attack? Can we be clearer about the purpose of life and the purpose of our relationships? Is it possible to heal our attitudes about ourselves and each other? Can we learn to live with integrity and honesty, without self-deception of any kind?

Is it possible to live our lives with the same concern for others as we have for ourselves, and to be focused on giving rather than on getting? Is it really possible to live in a way that we no longer blame others or condemn ourselves for the things that seem to go wrong and cause us to lose our peace of mind?

Can we learn to no longer be afraid of love and to learn how to forgive ourselves and each other? Is it really possible to let go of our fear of death and the belief that death is the end of life? Can we learn to be more gentle, tender, and kind to each other and ourselves? Can we let go of all fear and give unconditional love to all others, without exception?

Is it possible to enjoy peace of mind even though we believe that life has been unkind and that there are many people who have hurt us? Can we feel peaceful inside no matter what is happening in the outside world?

In this book we answer all these questions with an unqualified and enthusiastic "Yes!" Together we will be exploring how the Principles of Attitudinal Healing can bring us peace of mind in every aspect of our lives. We will be looking at attitudes and concerns that come up in parenting, education, healing, aging, business, law, and much more.

We will be talking about everyday problems that all of us experience. We will discuss how attitudes can be healed whether you are acting as the provider or receiver of a service, a customer in a store or a salesperson, the manager of a large company or an employee.

We will be looking at both sides of every situation, with an emphasis on what we can do to feel at peace with one another rather than alienated.

Everywhere we go, we are finding that whether one is the president of a powerful organization, or a secretary, nurse, lawyer, bus driver, physician, police officer, housewife or househusband, teacher, student, child, or adult, there is frequently a yearning, deep within, to experience a sense of inner peace, a tranquil mind, and a sense of being joined with others.

In a very real way this book is about that deep inner yearning, a yearning for spiritual fulfillment in all our lives. It is about honoring our humanness and the indomitable spirit of love that lives inside us all.

This is a book about the practicality of love and forgiveness, two of the most powerful forces in all our lives. We have tried to present a pragmatic spirituality, a nuts-and-bolts, not pie-in-the-sky approach to life, showing how spiritual principles such as love, forgiveness, compassion, kindness, and gentleness really can help us accomplish the challenges of our everyday lives with inner peace and love.

The principles we have described here are about seeing every encounter, even those that seem filled with great conflict, in another way, a way that brings peace of mind and a sense of joining, rather than fear and a sense of separation.

This is a book about learning to be spiritually fulfilled, finding harmony between body, mind, emotions, and spirit, and a comfortable balance between inner and outer success.

It is a book about retraining our minds, opening our hearts to intimacy, and learning to listen to the inner guide that each of us has within our hearts. It is about trust, faith, and hope. And it is about finding purpose in our lives and making a positive difference in the world.

After you read this book, it is our sincere desire and hope that whenever you might find yourself in conflict, you will know that a solution can come by changing your mind and changing your life.

PART I

❖

CHANGE YOUR MIND

❖

CHAPTER ONE

WHAT IS ATTITUDINAL HEALING?

Perhaps the biggest gift
that humankind has been given
is the choice to decide
what thoughts and attitudes
we put in our minds.

RESISTANCE TO CHANGE

When a friend or a person at one of our lectures or workshops asks us to describe the principles of Attitudinal Healing, I (Jerry) often think of the example of my own life and how certain beliefs that I have held in my mind came very close to destroying me.

From 1925 to 1975, the first fifty years of my life, I felt that I was the victim of my own faulty attitudes and bad habits. And try as I might, I did not seem to be able to change either my very critical thoughts about myself or my behavior.

I felt unlovable, and no one could convince me otherwise. Although there was part of me that wanted to change, there was another part that strongly resisted any kind of change. I felt that if I dared to open myself up and become vulnerable, people would find out what I was really like, ensuring that I would be rejected.

I seemed locked in a battle with myself, and that battle frequently resulted in provocative behavior that made it very difficult for other people to be in my company. I hated myself and was paralyzed with the fear of being rejected. Although I might have looked tough on the outside, my heart felt weak and wounded, and I continued to build a sharp picket fence around it so that others could not get close to me. I underwent many kinds of psychotherapy. I even tried psychoanalysis, but nothing seemed to work for me.

It was as if my attitudes, my behavior, and my habits were locked in a vise or stuck in cement. I had convinced myself that I was incapable of changing and that I was doomed to a life of failure. This became my belief, and I succeeded in making myself right by continuing to see myself as a failure. This resulted in my being unforgiving to myself and others.

As I look back on it, I can now see that my negative and

fearful attitudes about myself penetrated every area of my life. Although I attained great success professionally—as the world measured it—my inner life was anything but successful, filled with conflict and chaos.

My attitudes were like dark shadows that followed me everywhere I went, playing havoc with my schooling, in sports, and in my role as a parent and spouse. These attitudes played a painful role in my relationships with legal professionals during my divorce proceedings. My fear, along with my unforgiving and unloving attitudes toward myself, seemed unshakable.

I was scared of love and intimacy. I was afraid that I would be hurt. With thunderclouds of guilt I vacillated between finding fault with myself and finding fault with others. I seemed to be most unsuccessful whenever I tried to control people and events around me. So many of my thoughts were centered on the idea that I was a victim of things outside of myself.

I realize now that I was not alone in how I looked at the world. There are many others who go through life with feelings just like the ones I described.

A COURSE IN MIRACLES

In 1975—during a period when I was destroying myself with alcohol—I felt that I was beyond any help. I was a militant atheist and not the least bit interested in anything spiritual. It was then that a miracle happened to me. My friend Judith Skutch Whitson gave me a copy of an unpublished manuscript entitled "A Course in Miracles." The Course is about the power of love and forgiveness and how these offer us everything we could possibly want. As I became a student of the Course, my life began to change dramatically, and it began to take on a totally different meaning and purpose.

I began to discover that it was not my behavior that needed changing. What needed changing were my thoughts, my beliefs, and my attitudes. As I recognized that it was my thoughts that created my reality, I found that healing my attitudes began to create a new reality for me. When I started letting go of my attachments to fear and guilt and became more focused on "giving" rather than "getting," I also started to experience an inner peace that until that time I never would have thought possible.

As my "me first" attitude began to dissolve, I took a leap of faith and made the choice to trust in a Higher Power to direct me. I began to experience the power of love and forgiveness bringing me happiness. Relationships that I thought might never be healed began to be healed. As I let go of my compulsion to control others and let God direct me, miracles of love began to happen in my life.

WHAT IS ATTITUDINAL HEALING AND HOW DOES IT WORK?

Attitudinal Healing is based on the belief that it is not people or conditions outside ourselves that cause us to be upset. We are not victims of the world we see. Rather, what causes us conflict and distress is our own thoughts and attitudes about people and events. Further, we are not only responsible for our own thoughts, we are responsible for the feelings we experience, and through exploring these feelings we can eventually heal them.

Attitudinal Healing involves correcting our misperceptions and removing the inner obstacles to experiencing peace. This begins with having a willingness to find another way to look at the world, at life and at death—to have peace of mind as our only goal and the willingness to forgive as our main function. It is discovering the value we have placed on holding on to grievances, blaming others, or condemning ourselves, then making new choices to no longer find value in them.

In Attitudinal Healing we believe that the purpose of all communication is joining, not separation, that happiness is a choice, and that our natural state is one of harmony, creativity, and happiness. We create the disharmony and unhappiness we experience because of the attitudes we hold in our minds. The separation we experience in our lives comes from projecting these thoughts and feelings onto people and events outside us. We begin to heal that sense of separation when we strive to ask ourselves, in all of our encounters: "Is this communication for joining or separation?" and "Do I want to be happy or do I want to be right?"

Attitudinal Healing is a retraining of the mind and an opening of the heart, removing whatever blocks love's presence. It leads to freedom rather than bondage. Attitudinal Healing is about teaching and demonstrating love, not fear, in both our professional and personal lives.

Attitudinal Healing is based on the belief that it is possible to choose peace rather than conflict and love rather than fear. It is based on the belief that love is the most important healing force in the world.

Attitudinal Healing is a process for letting go of painful, fearful attitudes. When we let go of fear, only love remains.

As we begin to apply these principles throughout our lives, we find it helpful to think of "health" as inner peace and "healing" as the process of letting go of fear.[1] This process is based on the premise that each instant provides us with a new opportunity to reexamine our lives and to once again choose what it is we want to experience—love or fear, peace or conflict.

The term *Attitudinal Healing* came into being when we started the first Center for Attitudinal Healing in Tiburon, California, in 1975.

The Center for Attitudinal Healing

Not long after becoming introduced to *A Course in Miracles*, I became concerned with the plight of young children who were facing catastrophic illnesses and the possibility of death. I had noticed that children in hospitals often did not seem to have anyone to talk with about these problems. I felt an inner direction to start a small center where these children could come to have their own support group. We called it the Center for Attitudinal Healing. It would be a center where no fee would be charged for direct services, and to this day that policy continues. In the beginning the Center worked only with children who were facing life-threatening situations. Later we extended the program to siblings and parents and after that to adults with catastrophic illnesses, to people wishing to heal their relationships, and even to those with AIDS. We have "pen pal" and "phone pal" support networks—all guided by the principles for Attitudinal Healing.

Even though the Center started out working only with children, we found that the same principles carried over into every area of our lives—in healing our relationships with ourselves and in ending the battles that so often go on in our minds.

Guided by the principles, most of the people who work at the Center go through important transformations in their lives. Out of the sorrow and grief that they might experience, there is frequently an unfolding of a new spiritual awareness. They find themselves wanting to serve others and help them through their difficulties, which in turn helps them through their own. They discover that giving and receiving are the same. They become witnesses, allowing others to see and trust that there truly is another way to look at life and death.

PRINCIPLES OF
ATTITUDINAL HEALING

The twelve principles that we developed at the Center are now being utilized at the more than eighty-five independent centers throughout the world. The principles begin with the belief that the essence of our being is love and that our true identity is a spiritual one. These principles lead us away from fear and toward the reality of love in every moment of our being. They are helpful in leading us along the pathway of experiencing spiritual transformation in our lives. All the principles blend into the first one—that the essence of our being is love. Forgiveness is the underlying theme of all the principles.

By following the principles of Attitudinal Healing we learn that it is possible to heal our sense of separation, our fearful feelings, and any lack of peace we may be experiencing in our lives. We do this by remembering that our true identity is love and that every one of us is a spiritual being. Healing comes the moment we remember that our only purpose is to give our love and be kind, compassionate, and helpful to each other.

The principles of Attitudinal Healing are statements that allow us to look at the world and to perceive it differently. They are designed to help us let go of the ego's attachment to fear, anger, and "attack thoughts" in order to allow love to flow freely and uninterrupted into and through our lives.

To change our beliefs, we need only to make the decision to have a little willingness to look at our lives differently. By changing our thoughts and our attitudes, we can change the world that we experience.

The following are the twelve principles of Attitudinal Healing that have grown out of the work at the Center. We have included brief explanations of each that hopefully will make them clear to you.

1. THE ESSENCE OF OUR BEING IS LOVE.

This first principle is based on the premise that our true identity is as spiritual, not physical, beings and that our essence is love.

As simple as this sounds, there is a part of us that resists it. This resistance comes from our believing that we should fear love and not trust in it. It tells us that we must believe that we are only bodies, born to die, and that the death of the body is the end of us.

This principle, telling us that the essence of our being is love, is the key to Attitudinal Healing. As you read the remaining principles, you will find that this first principle flows throughout all the rest.

2. HEALTH IS INNER PEACE. HEALING IS LETTING GO OF FEAR.[2]

We live in a world where the word *health* is usually associated with the state of our bodies. In Attitudinal Healing health is focused not on the body but on the mind. It is based on the premise that our natural state of mind is inner peace. We can have inner peace regardless of the state of our body or what is happening in our outside life. Even a person who is dying of a disease such as cancer or AIDS can have this inner peace. Healing is letting go of fear—because letting go of fear leads directly to our having a peaceful mind, filled only with loving and peaceful thoughts, and experiencing that peace in all aspects of our life.

3. GIVING AND RECEIVING ARE THE SAME.

The world is often viewed as a very unfair, unfriendly, and unloving place where it is important to get as much as you can and to hold on to it. Our belief is that when we give something to another person, we then have less than what we had before, like taking money from our pocket and throwing it into a fire. It believes in getting, not giving, or in giving in order to get.

This principle is based on the belief in abundance, not scarcity. The Law of Love is like a boomerang, so all that we give comes back to us in a variety of shapes and forms.

4. WE CAN LET GO OF THE PAST AND THE FUTURE.

We are convinced that one of the reasons many of us are so tired, weary, irritable, angry, and depressed is that we spend inordinate amounts of time each hour of every day and night focused on the hurts and unforgiving thoughts of the past; we are afraid that we are going to be hurt, rejected, or unloved again and are fearful of the future because we believe that the awful past is doomed to repeat itself.

When this is our belief, we find that it is impossible to be happy in the present. As a matter of fact, many of us spend so much time brooding about the past and being afraid of the future that we allow ourselves to spend hardly any time in the precious present. Instead we spend our time superimposing the past upon the present.

When we see no value in hanging on to unforgiving thoughts and the hurtful past, we then can let go of the past.

When we begin to see no value in being preoccupied with a fearful future, we can let go of it.

We can put all our energies into extending love in the present. Most of us believe that what happened to us in the past is still affecting us today. What is actually happening is that our past experiences, where we believed we were victims, no longer exist and therefore can no longer affect us. All that remains are the thoughts, attitudes, judgments, and perceptions we have about those experiences; these do continue to affect us. But since we make all these in our minds, we do have choices about whether we will continue to hold on to them or let them go.

5. Now Is the Only Time There Is . . . and Each Instant Is for Giving.

Our everyday experience is based on a belief in linear time, and that time is for performing, judging, condemning, and of course worrying. So often we believe that we should be selfish and self-centered and think of ourselves first. It would want us to worry about being secure in the future and to trust no one completely—not others, not ourselves, and certainly not God or a Higher Power.

This principle suggests that there is another reality that is not based on linear time, and that it is possible to live each second as if it were the only time there is, an eternal, loving, giving view of time where there is no rush or hurriedness.

6. WE CAN LEARN TO LOVE OURSELVES AND OTHERS BY FORGIVING RATHER THAN JUDGING.

We are often focused, like laser beams, on what bodies do and what they are for. They are constantly being judgmental—either blaming others or condemning ourselves. Many of us have a firm belief that people do unforgivable things and that our safety lies in never forgiving or forgetting how others may have injured us. It is this belief that destroys our peace of mind and our health.

Because we project our own anger onto others, the process of forgiving others leads to the process of forgiving ourselves. We cannot totally experience ourselves as love until we have totally forgiven all others and ourselves.

Learning to let go of the blocks to loving, and forgiving others and ourselves, reminds each of us that the essence of our being is love. Perhaps we could consider that our real purpose in life on earth is to love ourselves and others by forgiving.

7. WE CAN BECOME LOVE FINDERS RATHER THAN FAULT FINDERS.

When we experience separation in our relationships it is because we are feeling that we must find fault in other people. However, our spiritual being sees relationships as a way of finding love—which results in joining. It teaches us that it's really much easier to love than to hate.

8. WE CAN CHOOSE AND DIRECT OURSELVES TO BE PEACEFUL INSIDE REGARDLESS OF WHAT IS HAPPENING OUTSIDE.

Our past experiences often frighten us into believing that everything that happens to us is caused by conditions, people, or events outside ourselves. We subsequently believe that we are always in danger of being attacked, hurt, and victimized.

This principle helps us to see that there is another way of looking at the world and that our own thoughts cause and create our own reality. It is based on the principle that it is not people or conditions outside of ourselves that cause us to be upset, but rather that our distress is caused only by our own thoughts about those things.

This principle leads us to freedom by reminding us that it is only our thoughts about the world that cause our distress. It reminds us that every second of our lives we can have inner peace regardless of the chaos that may be going on around us.

9. WE ARE STUDENTS AND TEACHERS TO EACH OTHER.

Many of us have been taught to believe that wisdom comes only from years of experience and age and that teachers have something to profess and nothing to learn from their students.

However, when we begin to recognize that there is a student and teacher in each of us, our perspective changes. We start to understand that each of us has something to learn from the other, and that everyone is an equal teacher regardless of age or "credentials." When the student is ready, the teacher will appear. And vice versa!

10. WE CAN FOCUS ON THE WHOLE OF LIFE RATHER THAN THE FRAGMENTS.

During our lives we look at the world as if we were looking through a kaleidoscope, seeing tiny fragments, but never the whole. In actuality the world is like a fabric where everything and every living being is interwoven. When we can step back from a fragment of life and see it in relationship to the whole, we gain a new perspective and can therefore make brand-new choices.

11. SINCE LOVE IS ETERNAL, DEATH NEED NOT BE VIEWED AS FEARFUL.

Rather than adhering to our belief that we are born only to die, this principle points out that when we truly believe that love is eternal, we will not be afraid of death. When we are no longer afraid of dying, we can truly begin to live.

12. WE CAN ALWAYS SEE OURSELVES AND OTHERS AS EITHER EXTENDING LOVE OR GIVING A CALL FOR HELP.

When we choose to change how we perceive others in this world, when we see them as either loving or fearful, giving a call of help for love, we are home free. On the other hand, if we continue to persist in the belief that "attack" comes from outside, we will always find a way of rationalizing or defending ourselves and attacking back. Rather than perceiving others as attacking, we can learn to see them as fearful.

When we respond to what we perceive as another's attack by seeing that person as fearful and giving a call of help for love, instead of defending ourselves or attacking back we get in touch with a very different place within ourselves. Our response to the other's attack generates love rather than more fear, no longer perpetuating the game of attack and defense.

• • •

We always have a choice about how we look upon these principles. For example, we can choose to look upon them as a bunch of idle words, hollow in their meaning.

OR: We can choose to apply them in every area of our lives, thus determining for ourselves whether they are empty words or are actually helpful and meaningful. As we learn to apply these principles, it may be helpful to ask, "Do they help me experience peace or conflict?"

THERE IS ANOTHER WAY

The first step in Attitudinal Healing is to "have a little willingness," just as we often suggest to people to have an open mind and to consider the possibility that there is another way of looking at the world. To do this, we are encouraged to take a fresh look at all the beliefs and values that we have been holding so dear to our hearts and to determine if they are really helping us to feel more peace and love.

When we believe that our thoughts and attitudes determine everything we see and experience, then what we see is what we believe. When we have fearful thoughts, we see a fearful world. When we have only loving thoughts in our minds and hearts, we see only a loving reality.

Truth can be defined as that which doesn't change. The highest form of that truth is love, a powerful expression of that which created us—call it God, Higher Power, or the Creative Life Force. Within this belief system our true identity is unconditional love, something that is never changing and that never dies. Another way of looking at our purpose is to remember that we are here to teach only love, for that is what we are.

In this other way of looking at the world we have a belief system that says that all the forms we see are but some aspect of our own thoughts being projected outward. What we project out into the world is what we perceive, and what we perceive is actually a mirror of the thoughts in our minds, not a fact or a truth.

It is as if the world is a giant screen in a movie theater, and what we see on the screen is but a projection of our thoughts and past experiences. What we see with our physical eyes and hear with our ears looks very real indeed. Unlike truth, which is constant and unchanging, what we see and hear is always changing.

Another way of looking at the world is to have the willingness to choose a way of life where peace of mind is our only goal, where forgiveness is our only function, and where we make decisions by quieting our minds and listening to the voice within our hearts telling us what to think, say, and do. It is living a life that focuses on giving rather than only getting, on serving others rather than just paying attention to our own selfish interests. It is living a life where our concern for others is the same loving concern we have for ourselves.

ATTACHMENTS TO FEAR, GUILT, AND ANGER

What keeps us from having inner peace is our attachment to fear, guilt, and anger. These have made us fearful of intimacy and feelings of love in all areas of endeavor. As we cling to patterns of fear, guilt, and anger in our thoughts and actions, we only make more confusion and chaos. Too often we find ourselves living our lives as if the only questions we have to consider are ones of pure survival. We are frequently consumed with fear and with what we think of as "justified" anger, that is, anger where we can point to something that has happened as "proof" that we must be angry.

We feel that perhaps there is nothing that blocks our awareness of love's presence more than fear, anger, and guilt. Our attachments to them have penetrated so deeply that there is not a single part of our lives that has been left uncontaminated by their presence.

How Our Egos Hide the Truth from Us

Our egos—or personality selves—try to convince us that we live in a world where the "cause" of everything that happens is outside us. Our experiences are then just the "effects." Our lives are nothing more than a series of responses to things that happen outside us as if we had no choice whatsoever in the matter. To be convinced that life really is that way, we must blot out all evidence that the world we see is determined by our own belief systems and the thoughts we hold in our own minds. This way of thinking can only last as long as we continue to be attached to the idea that we have nothing to do with creating the world we experience. We insist that we are only bodies, meant to be here for a brief period of time and then to die, with that being the end of life.

We spend a lot of time trying to figure things out in a very complex world based on the belief in fear. We seek security even as we are constantly telling ourselves to live in fear, that somehow we will be hurt in some way. We become attached to the belief that we must look but never find what we are seeking—and if we do find something, to know that it is never enough.

When we live according to this fearful belief system, we frequently feel we are victims and are constantly looking for someone to name as our enemy. This belief system seems to be telling us that there will always be wars, that the past will always predict the future, that you cannot trust love, and that others, and even ourselves, have done things that are unforgivable. This belief system would have us hold on to the idea that guilt and punishment are valuable—which they are not.

It is so very important to respect the power of our thoughts. After all, it is our thoughts that make our behavior and determine how we see the world and react to it. In the thought system of fear it is okay to have "attacking thoughts" because only "attacking actions" can harm other people.

Another way of looking at the world is to believe that our

thoughts can be just as harmful as our actions. The world we see begins to change when we let go of all our attack thoughts and replace them with loving thoughts.

HEALING THE PAST

There is a part of each one of us that resists change, even change that promises to make our lives better. Our resistance to change and our attachment to fear can make the Principles of Attitudinal Healing seem anything but easy at first. But by focusing our attention with many daily reminders that tell us there really is another way of looking at the world, we find peace rather than conflict and see that we really do have a choice.

It is clear that most of us want to experience loving and trusting relationships and to feel in harmony with each other and with the world in which we live. What seems to prevent us from this experience is the fact that so many of us keep the fires burning on the coals of our past dismal experiences. This results in our feeling fearful and hopeless about the future. The unhealed past and our belief that the past will repeat itself make us feel limited and immobilized.

Through Attitudinal Healing we explore ways to heal the past and rekindle hope in our hearts. We begin to experience our lives as useful and meaningful. We explore the thoughts that guide us in healing our feelings of isolation, loneliness, and separateness. We learn to heal our false beliefs that we are unloved and unlovable.

As we continue to focus on spiritual pathways, with the belief that the solution to all our problems is love and forgiveness, we find that it gets easier to resist the temptation of believing that we are unloved and unlovable. Needless to say, there are still plenty of days in our own (Diane and Jerry's) lives when we are not successful in this and we end up with anger and blame, perceiving ourselves as attacked. More and more, however, we are realizing, along with so many others, that how we see the world, and what emotions and attitudes we have, are at some level our own choices.

Through the principles of Attitudinal Healing it becomes clear that when we are willing to see the world differently, when we choose to see other people not as attacking us but as being fearful and giving a call of help for love, we discover compassion and inner peace. The change that takes place within anyone who makes this choice allows her or him to be more successful at forgiving and loving.

We feel that today there is more and more awareness that within each of us is the capacity to determine the thoughts we put into our minds. And it is really this ability that offers us the road to freedom from what, for so many of us, will eventually be revealed as a self-imposed prison.

In the chapters that follow, we have tried to share with you some of the many teachings that we have had the opportunity to experience. What we will be sharing here are real stories of real people and how they used the principles to help them in their lives. In every case we have attempted to get people to tell, in their own words, exactly how the principles had helped them so that others might see ways to apply those lessons in their lives.

It is our hope that, like us, you will find these stories helpful and that the lessons these people have learned, and now share with us, will bring as much peace, caring, and love into your life as they have into ours.

Some months before the publication of this book, we received a letter from Kaycee Poirier, who lived in Canada at the time. She was ten years old and had a brain tumor. After reading our principles of Attitudinal Healing she had written to us saying that she felt that they were good but they were not written in a child's language. She rewrote them for us, stating that, "This is my gift to other children who are fighting to live."

Kaycee died before she could see her writing in print. But before she died we wrote to her and expressed our heartfelt thanks. It is with great joy that we wish to share her edited version of the principles with you. Perhaps there is a child in your life who would like to share them too.

**The Children's Version of the
Twelve Principles of Attitudinal Healing**

1. Love is one of the most important things in life!
2. It is important to get better—so we must not let fear trap us!
3. Giving and receiving are the same thing.
4. Don't live in the past and don't live in the future.
5. Do what you can now. Each minute is for giving love.
6. We can learn to love ourselves and others by forgiving instead of not forgiving. Example: fighting.
7. We can find love instead of fault.
8. If something is the matter outside, don't go crazy, because you are safe inside.
9. We are students and teachers to each other.
10. Don't just look at the bad things, look at the good things too!
11. Since love is forever, death need not be scary.
12. We can always see other people as giving love or asking for help.

A Note to Our Readers About the Center for Attitudinal Healing

Since we have found in the past that many of our readers want to know more about the Center for Attitudinal Healing, we felt it might be helpful to include the following information:

People come to the Center from all different faiths and cultural backgrounds.

All support-group services at the Center in Tiburon, California, are free. There are currently close to one hundred centers located throughout the world, and you can consult the individual center nearest you for descriptions of their services. There have been numerous books for adults and children that have been written about the work at these centers. There are also a number of video and audiotapes that are available.

The Center in Tiburon offers for a low fee five three-day workshops each year on Attitudinal Healing. If you desire further information about the Center's work and workshops, please write to the Center for Attitudinal Healing, 19 Main Street, Tiburon, California 94920. Telephone (415) 435-5022.

❖

CHAPTER TWO

ATTITUDES ABOUT LIVING AND DYING

Perhaps our greatest underlying fear,
which permeates all our problems,
is the fear of death and separation.

WHEN THE STUDENT IS READY, THE TEACHER WILL APPEAR

In 1971 Helen, a fifty-five-year-old woman who had been a patient of mine (Jerry), called me on the phone and told me that she was dying of cancer. She asked me if I would be willing to be with her and talk with her as she went through her dying process. I had to stop and think about how I would answer that question. I finally explained to her that this was not my area of expertise, and I had my own unresolved fears about death. However, I assured her that I would be willing to help in any way I could.

At that moment I had no way of knowing what a powerful teacher this woman would become for me. But since that day I have had many occasions to find out that when we are ready to learn, a teacher will appear. I now know that when Helen called me that day, I had come to a time in my own life when I was ready to look at death.

Over the next two months I visited Helen in the hospital nearly every day. On the days when I didn't see her, we spoke on the phone. She was a very religious person and had an unwavering faith and trust in God.

I have to say that I really didn't know how to help her. I felt inadequate because of all my own unresolved issues around death. As time went on, however, I found there was something I could do with great confidence. I saw that my job was to give my love to her unconditionally and to listen to her without any judgment. I knew I was just to be with her. Having been a *doer* all my life, I can assure you this was something very foreign to me.

Helen talked about everything imaginable. I cannot think of a subject we didn't touch upon. Most of the time she really did not seem fearful of dying—but there were certainly times when she had doubts. There were tears, of course, but there was also much laughter. And at times there was anger too.

Most of the time I was amazed at the great calm and tranquility I felt in her presence. Unlike me at that time, Helen believed that we are more than just our bodies. She believed that her soul, her spirit, would live forever, never to be touched by death. She felt that she was always connected to God and would never be separated from the hearts of everyone she loved. Helen told me that she didn't believe there was any such thing as separation.

Helen died in her sleep one night, slipping away very peacefully. With all my heart I envied and admired her for having such unwavering faith and trust in a Higher Power. She saw death as merely stepping aside and letting go of the physical body as she went back home into the light.

THE SPLIT MIND

My experience with Helen was split-minded, however. Part of me could see that there was another way of looking at death than the one I held on to in my own life. I could not deny the fact that I had witnessed a person who was not afraid to die. But there was another part of me that said, "There is no scientific evidence of anything after your body dies. Don't be taken in by this experience."

My behavior around this period of my life reflected my split mind. I was an alcoholic, and I was literally killing myself with booze. On one hand I remained fearful of dying. On the other, like so many other lost souls, I was drinking myself into an early grave.

WHAT IT IS LIKE TO DIE

A burning question that we ask ourselves over and over, whether we are children or adults, is What happens to us when we die? Can anyone prove whatever that answer might be? Do we live all of our lives uncertain about the future, even at the point of death?

And the answer has much to do with whether we consider ourselves to be physical beings or spiritual beings. This is brought into focus by an old story that Tony De Mellow used to tell about a man who goes to the parish priest and asks, "When I die, my body will be in the grave and my soul will be in heaven, but where will *I* be?"

A few years after my experiences with Helen I was making rounds at the children's cancer ward at the University of California Medical Center in San Francisco. I happened to overhear an eight-year-old patient ask his physician, "What is it like to die?" The doctor avoided the question and quickly changed the subject. It was then that I asked myself, What happens to kids when they really want to talk about confusing things that are bothering them, like death, and the adults around them have not yet dealt with this themselves?

After a little investigation I found that children usually look for someone they can trust and who will give them honest answers. Sometimes it's the person who comes to clean the room. Or maybe it's the night nurse, or someone the child senses would give them a direct reply. The little boy who asked the doctor, "What is it like to die?" opened up a door within me, a door to my own inner child that was still afraid to ask that question.

Through that encounter on the children's cancer ward that day I was guided to start the first Center for Attitudinal Healing, founded in 1975. Because of that one little boy's question, something within me said that if I started a center where children facing death could come and ask their questions, not only would they be able to help each other but they also would help me to look at death in a different way. I knew that the healing of my attitudes toward death would have to be experiential, not just intellectual.

In the many years that have followed, all of us at the Center have learned much about living and dying and looking at it all in a very different way. Sometimes it is almost as if the children and adults who have come there, most of them facing death themselves, have been like angels sent to be our teachers. We are convinced that many of the children we have seen are old souls in young bodies, here to teach us simple spiritual truths.

FEAR OF DEATH

Over the years the children and many others who have come to the Center have revealed so much about our attitudes toward death and dying. We have learned from them that whether we are fully aware of it or not, our fear of death, which is really the fear of separation, is the greatest fear known to humankind. Ordinarily we do not talk about death very much in our society, as if by burying our fears in the caverns of our minds, we will somehow avoid death forever.

Our fears can be disguised in many different ways. One of the most common ways our minds play with this fear is by telling us that we must always try to control other people. So often this grows out of the fear of knowing that we cannot have the control we would need to have our bodies live forever. Sometimes our magical thinking, way down deep in our subconscious, tells us something like this: "By controlling other people maybe I can control death itself, so that I will never die."

At the Center we hear many stories told by people who have chosen to face their own fears about death. One story we have heard is about the man who, when picking up a newspaper, always turned to the obituary column first. Most people read the front page first, or maybe the sports page or the comics, but not him. When he was asked why he turned to the obituary column first, he said it was because he felt reassured not to find his own name there. In his own odd way this was his way of feeling that he had some control over death.

The children and adults at the Center have made it very clear that we will be fearful of death as long as we remain attached to our bodies as our only reality. Our fears will continue as long as we believe that past, present, and future are the only reality and that life and the body are the same.

We will be fearful as long as we hold in our minds the belief that we are born to be here on earth but for a brief time, only to die. We will be fearful as long as we identify with our body—and not with our spirituality.

There are a great many other things that somehow come to symbolize for us our fear of death. In our workshops we often find that many people have gone through divorces. So many of them remark that the end of the marriage was like death. The loss of a job or business can also appear to be like death. How we respond to these situations will depend on our belief systems. These situations provide us with new opportunities for becoming more aware of our belief systems and who and what we are, what is our purpose, and whether or not our lives involve more than a physical body.

As we ask questions about death and dying, it is important to remind ourselves that many of our attitudes and fears in this area are learned. To release ourselves from these fears, it can be helpful to examine some of the details about how those fears got started. We can do this by looking back into our own lives at the times when we first became aware of death.

PERSONAL REFLECTIONS

We all learn about dying in different ways and at different ages. The first time I (Jerry) became aware of death was when I was four years old. There was an elderly man who was our neighbor. He loved to work in his garden, and one day I noticed that he wasn't around anymore. I asked my parents what had happened to him.

There was a long silence, and my mom's and dad's faces took on expressions of horror, as if I had just said something terrible. Finally my mother mumbled hurriedly, "He died and went to heaven," then both of my parents rushed from the room.

Later that day I tried to get more answers from my parents. But when I pressed them with my questions, they said,

"People don't live forever. When they die, they go to heaven. That is all you need to know. Now, don't ask any more questions about it."

I don't remember ever having any thoughts or fears about death before that time, but the experiences of that day turned out to be a tremendous shock. I felt as if all my joy was sucked out of me. Until that moment I think I believed that my parents, my brothers Les and Art, and I would live forever. In some magical way I believed I would be a kid forever and everyone else would stay the age they were at that moment. Nothing would change. I had yet to develop the concept that people get older and eventually die.

In my family I learned that I got rewarded for not talking about my feelings. That was the rule you followed if you wanted to be a *good boy*. So I grew up stuffing a lot of my feelings deep inside me, withholding my emotions from myself and other people. Along with everything else, I learned to repress from my awareness the fact that we are not going to live forever. My fear of death became so deeply internalized, it was nearly invisible.

My effort to control my fears of death took many bizarre forms. At one point I developed the fantasy of having my body frozen when I died so that I could be brought back to life, sometime in the future, when someone learned how to make dead people come alive again.

As I grew up, I began to recognize that neither of my parents believed what they had told me about going to heaven after we die. They both believed that when you die, that is the end. When you die, you die, and that's it.

I was protected from thinking about death and asking too many questions by never having to attend a funeral until I was a teenager. This only intensified my belief that death must be a horrible thing, proving that I must do everything I could to control it. When I was in high school, however, a good friend of mine was killed in an auto accident. I became convinced that if there really was a God, he must be a cruel, not a loving god to allow such a thing to happen.

I was a pallbearer at my friend's funeral. After that what

little faith I had in a Higher Power completely disappeared, and I became a militant atheist.

Many of my fears about death and dying came from identifying very closely with my mother's fears. She had abundant fears. In fact I think she was one of the most fearful people I have ever known. One of the first fears I remember learning from her was her fear of water. Additionally, she was afraid that I would drown. Because I believed that these fears were real, I took many precautions to control them. For example, I remember taking swimming lessons and being the only kid at the pool wearing fully inflated water wings.

My mother was also fearful of high places, new situations, and driving in the car. She was surely the master of all backseat drivers. She had many, many phobias, which ran the gamut from fearing that she would be killed in a car to fearing that she might die of cancer.

I might add that my mom died just before she reached the age of ninety-eight years. Only in her last five years did her fear of dying begin to disappear as she became very open-minded in her thinking. She liked for Diane and me to tell her stories about our work with children and adults who were facing life-threatening illnesses. She admired the people we told her about, people who had such a strong faith and trust in a Higher Power.

Three years before she died, she surprised us by asking questions about reincarnation. She told us that she thought that young children who have a genius for music or other things must be demonstrating some form of reincarnation, that they were somehow carrying over into their present lives skills they had developed in previous lifetimes.

Toward the end of her life my mother also said that she had begun to have comforting dreams about my dad, Leo, who had died just a few years before, at the age of ninety-two. She told us, "In my dream Leo came to me with outstretched arms as I was trying to cross the road to reach him. He looked so happy, and the dream seemed so real!" As she shared this dream with us, her eyes filled with tears, and she suddenly seemed filled with a quiet joy as she spoke. She had many dreams of this kind that we feel helped prepare her for her own transition.

One of the biggest gifts Mom gave me in her last days was to let go of her physical body, dying peacefully in her sleep as I sat at her bedside very early one morning. Although she had not been facing any medical crisis that day, I had received a premonition that I should go to her that night and be with her. I had never before received inner guidance to stay the night with her in her room. I will forever be grateful that I listened.

MEDICAL SCHOOL

Medical school reinforced everything I had ever learned as a child about holding my feelings inside and not showing any emotions, especially when it came to the subject of death. In those days a medical student was taught that to be a good doctor, you had to be objective at all times. You never let yourself be loose with your emotions.

Where death was concerned, we intellectualized and depersonalized the experience, basically stuffing our feelings. We not only cut our feelings off from our patients, we cut them off from ourselves.

BEING FULLY ALIVE OR LIVING AS IF YOU ARE HALF DEAD

As I (Jerry) look back on much of my life, it is my impression that I spent a lot of my time walking around as if I were half dead. What do I mean by this? When we feel half dead, we are consciously or subconsciously worried about death and separation. We reinforce our fears of separation by judging and blaming others and condemning ourselves. We fear rejection, illness, and loss. We try to control others in a world that to us often feels insane and out of control.

We are frequently overcome with a sense of weariness

and exhaustion and never feel really secure. We hold on to hurt feelings from the past and we worry about the unknown future. We find it difficult, indeed, to trust anyone else— because we do not even trust ourselves.

We are half dead when we are afraid of love and intimacy. And we are half dead when we go around looking for something or someone outside ourselves to give us lasting happiness and joy. We are half dead when no matter what we get, it never seems to be enough. We are half dead when we do not believe in love.

To us, being fully alive means being one hundred percent in the present; looking beyond the world of form as the only reality; being totally filled with love and the spirit of giving; having no fear of death; having no limits; being totally connected and joined to all that is; being free of judgments; experiencing joy, happiness, and peace in the present; and having no attachments to physical bodies or time.

Most people have at least had moments when they experienced themselves as being fully alive. If you are anything like us, the problem is stringing those brief moments together into a continuous chain. This may be one of our greatest challenges in life, to choose to live *one second at a time*, to love rather than to fear, to choose to be fully alive rather than half dead.

BELIEF SYSTEMS

We do not believe that anyone could continue to work at our Center unless he or she was on some kind of spiritual pathway and believed that people's identity is more than just their bodies. If we believed that the death of the body was the end of the line, it would be just too painful to get close to children and their families at the time of death.

We are not saying that those of us at the Center do not suffer pain or grief when someone dies. We do. And we mourn the loss of the physical presence of those who have died. There is, however, a willingness to see life and death differently than we previously did—to see the possibility that life and love are eternal. We concentrate on attempting to see each other as spiritual beings who are never separated and are always joined with each other through love.

When you are under three, it is much easier to believe that this is the only time there is and that what you are will be here forever, because you have not learned the concepts of time, such as "yesterday" and "tomorrow." It is therefore easier to think that now is forever. Perhaps it is when we learn the ego's perception of time that we begin to be locked into our fear of death and the belief that death is final.

IMAGINING A DIFFERENT REALITY

Would you be willing, for just a few moments, to let your imagination run wild? Imagine how it would be to live in a world where everyone shared the belief that all perceptions of time—particularly the past and the future—were just beliefs, perceptions that we had invented. Can you imagine living in a world where the *here and now* is eternal? Would you be willing to imagine a reality where you always live in the present, with no thoughts about the past or the future, and where love itself is our identity, not our physical bodies?

As our imaginations carry us in the direction of viewing the world in this way, we begin to see that we would have a lot less fear in that kind of world than we have in the one where we live today. The belief in separation and death would fade away and disappear because there would no longer be a belief in the ego's perception of life—that we are only bodies moving through space and linear time.

IS A BELIEF A FACT OR A CHOICE?

At one time in history most people believed the world was flat. For most people at that time, the perception of a flat world was a fact, not a belief. It was only after explorers like Christopher Columbus came along, challenging that belief, that people began to see that the flat world "fact" was really a belief, and a mistaken one.

How open-minded are we really? There are many of us who accept as fact the belief system taught by our society. Belief systems are choices, and most of what we take to be *beliefs* about time, our physical bodies, and death are really just that—beliefs. It can be helpful to remind ourselves that we really *can choose* what we believe and what we think, and to recognize that what we choose determines what we experience.

OTHER WAYS OF LOOKING AT LIFE AND DEATH

There are many other ways of looking at life and death than through the beliefs we learn in our own culture. I (Jerry) had the opportunity of attending a Maori Indian funeral in New Zealand a number of years ago. The service was taking place in a large hall and there were about a hundred people present, including many children. Everyone was in a happy, festive mood. At one end of the hall was an open casket containing the body of an elderly man who had died. Children were playing around the casket.

There was no fear, because death was not feared. The spirit of the man whose body was in the casket was being celebrated. It was believed that his spirit would live forever. I thought that if I had been brought up in this culture, I would have very different beliefs about death and I would not have been afraid of it.

During the same visit to New Zealand I met a seventy-five-year-old retired priest from the Catholic church. He told me that he was writing a book about the Maori. He felt that one of the biggest mistakes ever made was trying to convert these people. Instead of trying to change their beliefs, he believed we should have learned from them about their spiritual truths.

The Maoris' beliefs about their spiritual identity extend into every area of their lives. They have one word for "love";

it is *awara,* which means "unconditional love." They don't
believe in the concept of separation at all. If a person comes
to visit from a different place in the world, she or he is not
looked upon as a foreigner but is accepted as a part of their
family. There are no limitations placed on love. Everyone is
loved equally.

CHILDREN HAVE BEEN OUR TEACHERS

At the Center for Attitudinal Healing we have been impressed by how many of the children we have known had
a strong belief in a Higher Power, even those who had little
or no religious background. These children have often
seemed wise beyond their years when it came to their understanding about life and death. They often speak of walking into the light and they feel they are connected with a
Higher Power forever, that there is no separation, not even
in death.

We love the story of the ten-year-old boy who had come
close to death many times. One day he said to us, "I think
God has a library, and the books in the library are children.
These children are loaned out to parents and they all have
due dates on them. Like the books in the library, some books
have a short due date and others have a longer due date.

"The books are always part of God's heart, and although
they are loaned out, they never really are separated. So I
always feel joined to God and am not scared of dying. But
I think I have some more work to do here."

That boy told us these things over ten years ago. He is
still doing well and wants to do something with his life to
help others.

We also remember an eleven-year-old boy whose parents
had been quite religious but turned away from their belief
in God when the boy's cancer returned. The boy told his
parents, "What you believe is okay with me. But I really feel
God is with me all the time, and the fact that my cancer has
returned doesn't mean that God is gone."

We have gotten to know some children at the Center who

express no particular religious or spiritual beliefs yet their actions reveal a very different way of looking at the world. They find a sense of peace within themselves by being able to meet regularly with other children, to share their mutual problems and be of help to each other. Being helpful to others during their own crisis allows the children to feel a sense of purpose and also to experience the fact that they are not alone. Time and time again they express the belief that if you send love to someone who is in a hospital miles and miles away, that day they will receive that love. They believe that through the love in their hearts they can communicate with each other without their physical bodies having to be in the same place. They know in their hearts that when you are giving love, you do not feel alone or separate.

Elsie Hines

An outstanding example of a person who was not afraid of death was Elsie Hines. Her daughter, Linda Ryan, shared with us the following story about her mother.

"My mother had a very close relationship with God all her life. She believed that our true identity is a spiritual one, an eternal one. She was Catholic and not only prayed to God daily but also had a very close relationship to the Blessed Mother Mary. It was as if her faith in God had prepared her for death all her life. When she was seventy years of age, she was diagnosed with leukemia.

"Her physician wanted her to have chemotherapy, and she told him to wait three days and then she would let him know her decision. As with everything else in her life, she prayed to God for help in making her decision. Three days later she told her physician that she had decided not to have chemotherapy and explained that she had arrived at her decision through prayer. Her family was supportive of her in her decision, and her physician then followed in support as well."

Linda's mother began to discuss the kind of funeral she

wanted. She told Linda which clothes she wanted to wear. She also wanted her hairdresser to fix her hair in a certain way. Since it was going to be an open-casket funeral, she wanted her head to be in such a position that it would not show a lump she never liked on her nose; she even turned her head to demonstrate the exact position she wanted. Elsie had a wonderful sense of humor that continued just as sharp as ever through the last months of her life. It was during this time that Linda received one of the biggest and most blessed gifts she could ever receive from her mother. Her mother told her, "Linda, when I die, don't think that you never did enough for me, for you did!" Linda felt that this was one of the most liberating gifts any adult child could ever receive.

Later Linda's mother had to be in the hospital for a systemic infection, and she began to experience moderate pain. She made a decision to return home and stop receiving any more blood transfusions or pain medication. Upon arriving home, she sat in her chair and had some of her own homemade chicken soup that she had been storing in the freezer. That evening, after saying good night to her family, and praying with them, she pulled out her oxygen tube when her nurse, who checked her frequently during the night, left the room. When it was discovered what she had done, the nurse alerted the family members, who rushed to Elsie's bedside to say their last good-byes. Elsie had died in her own way. She couldn't wait to see the Lord and his blessed mother.

When we asked Linda if she could share with us what she had learned from her mother about dying, she replied, "My mother taught me that I have a lot of daily homework to do. She taught me to work hard, to let go of control, and to let God make my decisions. She taught me the importance of daily prayer and the peace that comes when you trust, have faith, and give your life to God."

Loss and Grief: A Chance to Heal and Grow

Teresa Spencer Plane, a dear friend of ours, lives in Australia. She has written the following piece entitled "Grief Is for Sharing: A Chance to Heal and Grow," excerpted from her own book, *Time to Come Home: A Guide for Families Living with Dying.* Because we have found it to be so extremely helpful to others, we would like to share some of its wisdom with you. The following comprises her thoughts, which we have edited in some areas—hopefully without changing her original intent:

GRIEF IS FOR SHARING

What does the grieving person need to know? What does he or she have to be able to do to work through the pain and chaotic emotions that accompany the death of a loved one?

To begin, we need to know that grief is a normal and natural response to loss. It is part of the human experience. Grief represents our humanness, as does our love. The death of a loved one is a universal experience, and its occurrence initiates a painful process from grief to healing. It is an unstable process, too, a lonely journey characterized by self-doubts and intense emotions.

The First Weeks

During the first few weeks and months you may feel you are living your life in slow motion. You may feel numb, detached from life, and unable to concentrate. Life is happening for others, but you may not feel part of it. You may feel that you have lost part of yourself. You feel disorganized and you may cry a lot. The sadness is overwhelming and you sigh frequently. Some people may feel they have to be strong and fight back the tears. Others feel that if they start to cry, they may never stop.

You may be very angry. Angry at God. How could God do this? There is no God. Angry at the world and those around you. Angry at yourself and even angry with the person who has died. How dare they die, leaving you so alone.

Loneliness is one of the biggest problems of grief—one feels abandoned and powerless.

Irrational guilt can sweep over you. Some may even feel a personal responsibility for the death.

Many find their grief to be exhausting. You feel tired all the time. Sleep is difficult; either we don't sleep or sleep is disturbed by vivid dreams and nightmares. While they may be distressing and indeed on occasions terrifying, in most cases these dreams will fade away in time.

You may find yourself talking to the dead person as if she or he was present. You come home from the supermarket and find you have bought a bottle of his usual shampoo or his favorite fruit juice. You may think you hear the dead person coming in the door and call out, "I'm in the kitchen," then realize no one is there, and the person will never walk through the door again.

If you swallow your grief, that proverbial lump in the throat will only surface later in the physical symptoms of insomnia, headaches, and gastrointestinal problems.

Left Alone

Some friends and even family members may not come to visit you after the funeral. They can often feel uncomfortable with your tears and intense emotions, and perhaps they don't know what to say. Others erroneously believe that their job is to distract you from your grief.

Talk About Feelings

Most grieving people need to speak about their feelings of grief, the loneliness, sadness, and depression, and "tell their story" to make living more tolerable. Talking about your loss in reality will help you to heal and work through the process of grief, so try to find people who will listen to you and help you feel understood and not alone.

In discussing grief it is important for each of us to remember we accumulate our losses. Every loss we ever encountered and suffered in our lives, if it has not been dealt with, is still with us. We are still carrying them.

Time Alone Does Not Heal

It is what you do with your grief that brings healing. It is important to remember that the length of time you grieve is not a sign of weakness. Each person will be unique in this respect.

UNDERSTANDING YOUR GRIEF

The full sense of the loss of someone loved never occurs all at once. The birthdays, wedding anniversaries, and the first anniversary of the death often make you realize how much your life has been changed by the loss. You have every right to have feelings of emptiness, sadness, despair, even guilt and anger. You may be frightened by the depth of emotion felt at these times.

Unfortunately many people surrounding you may try to take these feelings away, to "get your mind off your loss." But most people who have suffered a great loss need to speak about their feelings, the emptiness, sadness, and depression they are feeling.

There are many books that are helpful to those facing their own death or the death of a loved one, and there are many that discuss ways of dealing with loss and grief. However, these are all highly individualized processes, intensely unique for each of us. They are all processes we need to discover for ourselves.

We believe there is no way to prescribe how to die, how to live, or even how to grieve. However, we have often found that for those seeking their own way it can be helpful to hear the experiences of the many people who have come to the Center, who were guided by their desire to find answers for some of the same questions.

At the Center for Attitudinal Healing we have weekly group meetings on "Loss and Grief" for those people who want to process their feelings. Every month we also have an all-day session on the same subject, providing people with a safe environment for sharing their individual experiences.

People taking part in these groups attempt to listen without judgment to others' experiences and to offer their support. We would like to share some of the experiences we have had with people who have come to these meetings. Many were people who were facing their own deaths while others were dealing with loss and grief. And of course there have been a great many people at the Center who were doing both—facing their own deaths as well as grieving the loss of a friend they had met at the Center.

THE PAIN AND AGONY OF MOURNING

Many people have come to our Center who were unable to feel the full impact of their grief at the time their loved ones died. Many of them had obtained tranquilizers from their physicians to ward off the impact of the pain they were feeling at the time.

After taking part in the "Loss and Grief" meetings many of these people felt that it would have been much better not to have been on medication. They felt the drugs robbed them of the opportunity to explore and feel their own grief. After openly expressing their feelings in the safe setting these meetings offered, they emphasized the importance of going through their feelings about a loved one's death rather than covering these feelings up.

What most people discover is that regardless of the tranquilizer or other drug involved, the feelings of grief, anger, rage, loss, and deep sadness do not go away. They just get hidden away in their subconscious minds for a while, only to surface again at a later time, all mixed together in a very confusing way with other events and issues in their lives.

So many people have said that had they gone through the pain and agony of their own mourning process at the time of their loved one's death, it would have been extraordinarily helpful. It would have helped them climb another notch of their own learning ladder, allowing them to discover for themselves a little more about the mystery of life and death.

Many people talk about how important it has been for them to have a place where they can honor their human feelings and not feel that someone is judging them, criticizing them, trying to change them, trying to talk them out of what they are feeling, or thinking they are crazy for acting in a certain way. Groups like the ones we describe provide that.

One woman, for example, whose husband died suddenly in his sleep, continued to keep the same sheets on the bed for over a month before washing them. After sharing this with the group, she felt relieved when other people told her that they had done the same thing. It was helpful for her to know that there are no right or wrong ways to express one's grief.

People in the Center's support groups find that there is great value in being able to share with others who are going through the same things—and to learn that you are not alone. This sharing helps take the fear away.

There are people who have identified with their grief so strongly that they think that their grief defines them. Talking with others helps them to be able to look at themselves differently. One thing that needs to be emphasized is that the Center offers people hope in that it gives them another way of looking at life, another way of looking at death, and gives them an opportunity to process their own pain and anger and grief so that they can ultimately learn from the experiences and heal.

Today there are support groups of this kind in many cities throughout the United States, and in other countries as well, all offering support in the grieving process.

LETTING GO OF THE FEAR OF DEATH

Although we have no pet formulas for letting go of the fear of death, there are a number of things we've observed with those who have let go of that fear. We would like to share some of these observations with you.

One thing they all seemed to have in common was a willingness to question and reevaluate their old belief systems—not to have them "cast in concrete" or to attempt to discredit new experiences because they didn't fit neatly into their old reality. The best way we could think of to communicate the insights that grew out of the "Loss and Grief" workshops was to interview people and ask them to tell their stories in their own words. Here are their stories:

Patsy Robinson

Patsy is one of the founders of the Center and has been associated with it since 1975. Her story illustrates the importance of dealing with our fears of death by giving ourselves permission to experience those feelings in a more complete way. She teaches us that when we do this, we open the doors for fully recognizing that our true identity is a spiritual one, and this realization releases us from the fear of our physical death.

Patsy has worked in every capacity at the Center, from volunteer to president of the board, so we felt that she would be an excellent person to interview. She told us, "As I look back, I realize that before we started the Center, I used denial to deal with my fear of death. It was not until I started helping others around their loss and grief that I discovered that I had hidden and not really dealt with my father's death, which had occurred years before.

"I was helping facilitate a 'Loss and Grief' workshop when all of a sudden unstoppable tears began to come out of me. The very people whom I thought I was there to help began to help me. I think that what happened to me happens to many others. As you are listening to other people go through the pain of their grief and sense of loss, you often discover your own grief."

Patsy said that the person that impressed her most since she had been at the Center was Joe Bauer, who had died of a brain tumor a number of years before. She said, "I remember the first night that Joe came to our meeting. He said that he had recently gone to a physician who diagnosed him as having an inoperable brain tumor. Joe's doctor told him he had only about two months to live. When Joe heard this, he told us, 'I fired him. I did not want to go to a doctor with that little optimism.'

"Joe lived for another three years. During that time he

spent almost all his time helping others and learning to stay in the present. He really demonstrated to others, including me, that when you concentrate on living in the present, the quality of your life is the highest. He taught us the tremendous value of so strongly living in the present that it becomes your only reality. The fear that he had when he first came to the Center disappeared, and he developed a wonderful sense of peace that he was generously able to share with others.

"Often it seems to me that when people develop a catastrophic illness, it gives them an opportunity to look at their life, to reevaluate their purpose and what they feel life is all about. For many it seems to be a wake-up call for beginning one's own spiritual path. And it seems to me that we ought to be able to hear that wake-up call without having to face a catastrophic illness.

"It is hard to put into words the many wonderful experiences I have had. What I can say is that I have had many wonderful teachers who have faced their own death or who have faced the death of a dear one. For myself, perhaps the most important thing I have learned is that death is okay and I know in the center of my being that I am more than a body and that it is my spiritual self that is real. The experiences at the Center have helped me let go of my old fears, for which I am forever grateful."

Cheryl Daniels Shohan

Cheryl's story is important to us because it is such a clear lesson in how spiritual transformation can unfold from even the deepest grief, confirming our true essence as love. Cheryl is a woman who experienced a very deep and grievous loss—deeper than any of us will probably ever know. Her story demonstrates how we can heal ourselves by helping and giving to others, even when we have suffered the kind of pain that Cheryl has suffered.

Cheryl was raised in the Jewish faith, and she remembers feeling as a teenager that when you die, that is the end of life. She held that belief for many years.

Cheryl married and had a daughter, whom she and her husband named Kamala. A few years later she had a second child, whom they named Tajin. When Kamala was nine years old, she was diagnosed as having bone cancer. After radiation treatment and chemotherapy, she got better. Three years after that Kamala's brother, Tajin, was diagnosed as having aplastic carcinoma. He died four months later.

Cheryl and her husband, Paul, went through pain, despair, and agony that few of us could even imagine. They had felt deeply depressed and angry with God after Tajin died. They felt that they were victims and that the whole universe had turned against them. It was then, when they felt that they could not endure any more pain, that Kamala became ill again. Doctors diagnosed her as having radiation-induced osteosarcoma. At the age of thirteen years, almost exactly a year after Tajin's death, Kamala also died.

Cheryl tells how, following Kamala's death, she felt that both her children were present. Their presence was so strong that she was convinced that it was not just her imagination creating them. She became convinced that there is another reality parallel to the physical one with which we are more familiar. Since that time she has had a strong belief in a spiritual reality. It is this that she feels has sustained her through her loss.

Since Kamala's death Cheryl has worked at the Center as a volunteer, a facilitator, and a staff person. She is currently director of Family Services and Home and Hospital Visitations. She has been intimately involved with many, many people—both children and adults—during their dying process.

To the families and friends of these people Cheryl has been a wonderful role model, being a person who has gone through perhaps what to most of us was one of the worst pains one can experience, the death of both her children. The people she has helped can look at her and know that here is a person who has suffered this pain and has come out the other side, functioning fully, with peace and hope in her heart.

When we asked Cheryl what she felt was most helpful to

her when she was working with people who were dying, she said, "To know that I am most helpful when I am not afraid.

"It is *being* with the person when I'm free to share my peace, unconditional love, and acceptance. Often it is letting them know that there is no right or wrong way to die and that how they are doing it is perfect because we all do it perfectly. It is a willingness to be there, to listen, to help them process their unfinished business. It is knowing that giving and receiving are the same. Most important, it is a willingness to see their light, which in turn reminds me to see my own."

Sharon Pair-Taylor

Sharon is the director of Adult Program Services and has been a valued member of our program since she came to the Center a few years after it opened. In working with both adults and children Sharon feels it is important to be completely present in order to tune in to what you can think, say, or do to be helpful.

She said, "I think the most helpful attitude for me to have is one of not intruding on the other person's privacy. There are many times when the persons you are with may invite you to help them explore their inner thoughts and their unfinished business. This is a most precious time, when both of you can experience oneness and joining in a way that is beyond words."

Sharon emphasized how important it is to be completely honest at all times and to not disguise our thoughts and feelings. Perhaps what most impressed us was the following: "It is clear to me that we do not know what is best for another person. In our workshops we try to remind people that we are not there to try to shape how another person should die. We are there to create an environment of unconditional love, so that there is freedom to talk about any subject—or not to talk at all."

She went on to say that "the experiences I have had are rich beyond words. In working at the Center I continue to learn more about life-death issues and to recognize that we are all students and teachers to each other. My own spiritual journey has been enhanced by witnessing the spiritual transformation that has taken place in so many people that we have come to know."

Meg Harmon

Meg Harmon is another dedicated staff member at the Center and as the director of Loss and Grief Services she has had the opportunity to be with many people who are facing death. Although Meg's Baptist background taught her that life is eternal, that was not a belief she had ever been able to fully accept.

Meg's experiences, like those of many others at the Center, changed her way of thinking about love and the passing of the physical body. Her own mother's death allowed her to get more fully in touch with that part of herself that is neither the physical body nor the ego. Her story is important because of the particularly poignant way she describes how this realization unfolded in her life.

At the end of her mother's life Meg realized that the only thing that was really important to her (the mother) was the love she had given and received from others. Meg goes on to say, "What I realized, in a very profound way that I never had before was that love is the most important healing force in the world. This event changed my life because I realized that my priority was to heal myself through the love that is in my own heart.

"I started letting go of self-judgment and began to make the experience of sharing love the most important thing in my life."

Meg's commitment to a spiritual path has only deepened since she came to the Center. When I asked her to describe another peak experience, she described the time she spent with Paul Dearborn, a close friend, whom she was with when he died of AIDS. They had spent many hours together as he approached death. Paul had not been able to talk that day, so Meg spent the time with him in silence.

Meg said, "I had an experience that allowed me to look past his body. There was absolutely no question in my mind that we were both seeing the depth of each other's souls as we continued to join at a very deep level.

"The love we experienced had nothing to do with the body, and it was an experience that reminded me once again that since love is eternal, it never dies. The body is just laid aside. Paul died a very peaceful death, and I was rewarded by my experience with him by continuing to feel his presence in my life in a very real way."

Dr. Elisabeth Kübler-Ross

For so many people it is their experiences around death that allow them to discover, beyond a shadow of a doubt, that we are much more than our physical bodies. Our fears of death can be very powerful. In fact our egos oftentimes tell us that we must not think about death or allow ourselves to experience anything about it. One of the people whose work has been particularly helpful in guiding us beyond our egos' false messages is Elisabeth Kübler-Ross. Her contribution has touched the lives of millions of people throughout the world, establishing her as the unchallenged leader in her field.

For many years Elisabeth has been not only a dear friend but the brightest of *light beams* for us and the millions of others whose lives she has touched. Perhaps more than any other single person in our generation she has helped to bring the subject of death out into the open. Her work has made it possible for those both in and out of the health professions to acknowledge their feelings about dying. Elisabeth has helped to create a way for all of us to explore who we really are.

We recently interviewed Elisabeth for this book. She told us that her interest in the problems of dying started when she was six years old. "I had pneumonia," she said, "and I shared my room with another child. No one came in and talked with us about anything. We talked with each other a little, but most of our conversation occurred nonverbally.

"One night before we went to sleep, there were no words spoken between us. Yet I felt there was a communication going on between our minds. As I look back on it, it was telepathic communication. She was telling me that she was going to die that night. When I woke up the next day, her bed was empty. She was gone. I later found out that she had indeed died. I felt her presence with me, and that day I knew for sure that we were more than bodies."

Elisabeth's workshops on death and the dying process emphasize the importance of experiencing our feelings. She states that many people come to the workshops who have suffered all kinds of abuse—emotional, physical, and sexual. Many of these people have found that being able to express themselves in a loving, supportive environment heals inner wounds that years of intellectual analysis have failed to heal.

"In our workshops," Elisabeth said, "it is truly experiencing all of the repressed emotions that is important. People can then make a decision to release them, to let go of them, and to no longer be attached to them. The light at the end of the tunnel then becomes brighter as we come closer to discovering who and what we really are."

When we asked her if she had any pet formulas about what helped people the most, she replied, "I don't believe there are any *cookbook* recipes leading to a recognition of our own spirituality. It is a long, hard process of going inside and of self-discovery."

A DREAM OF PASSAGE

So many times the deaths of our loved ones have much to teach us about the ways we are joined. How we deal with the bonds between us can be the source of conflict and pain within us, sometimes even resulting in physical symptoms and illness. However, as my (Diane's) own experiences have taught me, those bonds can also guide us to the joy that comes with a deeper understanding of our spiritual connections.

I have been a facilitator for one of the AIDS groups at the

Center since 1987. Although we have had some long-term survivors in the group, we have also lost many to AIDS. It is difficult for me to comprehend that after developing such close relationships with them, so many are dead. Each person's life and death has had a unique effect on me, and the richness of what I have learned from each of them will never leave me.

It has never been easy watching their bodies waste away. And yet their courage and their spirit have always been an uplifting force in my life. It was never my expectation that I would be working with people who were facing life-and-death situations. The challenge of facing one person's death is difficult enough, but facing the deaths of so many friends seems almost incomprehensible.

I had received much support from Jerry, the staff at the Center, and others, as I tried to experience all aspects of my own mourning process. As I look back, I know there were times when I kept my emotions outside my own awareness. One example of this is that I recently had a series of sore throats that I had not been able to completely rid myself of. I can now see that it was quite possible that the lump in my throat represented tears and grieving that I just hadn't yet allowed myself to experience and bring to a completion.

One night before going to sleep (on the eve of my birthday) I remember asking the universe for help with the deep-seated emotions that were causing me so much discomfort. That night I had a vivid dream. To me this was a dream of passage, in which I was able to experience the unmourned losses I had after the deaths of so many dear friends. In one portion of this vividly detailed dream I was in a large room with many people who were also mourning the loss of loved ones. A man got up in front of the group and read an anonymous poem that expressed what we were all feeling. I knew that I was the author of that poem, but I did not wish to let the others know this.

Upon awakening from this dream, I was able to record it in vivid detail, and then I wrote down the poem that had been in the dream. I called the poem "The Bridge." Both the dream and the poem proved to be very healing for me as the lump in my throat seemed to dissolve and the sore throats disappeared. I include the poem here in the hope that perhaps it will be helpful to others who also are dealing with the process of mourning the loss of a loved one.

THE BRIDGE

Alone—living in the glance of death's mask. There is a grayness in the air, on shadowed skin and in the minds as they darken, dimmer and dimmer each day.

Bright young lives—shining with pride and the joyful expression of their being here at this time to Light the way—bridge the differences between straight and narrow mindedness.

Engulfed in grief—death all around. Daily obituaries of friends and lovers, old acquaintances and—ourselves.

It seems sometimes that I'm not sure who died—them or me. I only know that their courage and anger, their confusion and pain, their tears and their resignations, are all mine too.

It was so easy to step back into the nothingworld of now as I would leave them each week, detaching the cables of my heart that connected us one by one.

They were never all removed, you know—detached as I may become in the fortress of my mind, the cables remain intact to keep us joined forever.

There was an indistinguishable time when the cables lay heavy, weighted with loss and hopelessness. I thought they were built to help support them.

Today I can see that they were built by us all to keep us forever connected—a roadway or bridge of sorts—strong a span as ever there was.

It stands permanently as plaques to pain from one world to the next, from discrimination and hatred and fear to acceptance and compassion and love.

I will gladly hold my end—as I know they will theirs in the otherworld of eternal time, a place of youthful beauty expressed from the Inner Self of us all.

We will keep the cabled structure in place—not only to bind us in memory remembering your existence alive, but to secure a place for others to go.

They can walk safely now—protected by the familiarity of others gone before—guided by the love from this side and beyond. Joined in the experience that we all, intermittently, walk the road together. Only the scenery is different.

I thank you for another rung on the stout structure. You have bridged me with more than you ever knew, yet perhaps know now. You have connected me with my own self, my own grief, my own loss and my own love.

THE MOST IMPORTANT GIFT OF ALL

Perhaps the most frequently asked question we hear is What can I do to be helpful to someone who is dying? The person asking this question is usually looking for things both to do and to say. He or she may be fearful of saying or doing the wrong thing.

It is never easy for us to answer this question because we really don't feel that it is possible for us to know what is best for other people. The best way we can respond is to suggest that answers come when we are still and go inside ourselves and then trust what we hear. And through that process we find answers that are a little different for each of us.

When we (Diane and Jerry) go inside ourselves in this way, we are often reminded that it is most helpful to recognize the person we are with as our teacher. He or she is there to give us an opportunity not only to be helpful but to look at our own internal dialogues about life and death.

We have found that the most important gift we can give another person is our inner peace and our unconditional love and acceptance. For both of us we find that to be fully present, with an open heart, is much more important than to have prepared ahead of time exactly the "right thing" to say or do.

What seems to be essential is our being, our presence with the other person. We continue to ask for inner guidance about what to think, say, and do. And we are impressed by how often we receive the following message, loud and clear: "Just be. There is nothing that needs to be said. Just be. And let go of all fear. There is nothing you need to do. Just be."

The power of love as you sit in the silence holding the hand of a loved one, friend, or patient who is dying is limitless. Sitting with another person, seeing only that person's inner light, can dissolve all perceptions of separation and aloneness and can bring about a joining for both people that never ends. When we are feeling self-doubt, we remind ourselves that everyone was born with a Ph.D. in love.

LOOKING PAST THE BODY

When someone in our life is dying, and their body is wasting away, it is not always easy to look beyond what we think of as their physical reality. But if we choose to, we can, regardless of the state of the body. We can always choose to see the light shining from the very center of that person's being instead of focusing on the outer wrappings of the spirit, which the body represents.

When we believe in our hearts that there is no separation and that as spiritual beings we are always joined to each other and our Source forever, our attachments to our bodies and our fears begin to diminish. With faith and trust we can then recognize that our reality is not limited to the body, which continues to change. What is real is changeless, and the only thing we know that doesn't change is the eternal love that created us.

Affirmations

1. There is another way of looking at death other than believing that it is the end of the line.
2. When I am feeling grief, I will face my pain and not deny it.
3. When I trust and have faith that love is eternal and always joining, I will not believe in separation or death.
4. When I choose to believe that minds always communicate and that you do not need bodies to communicate, I will know that I can never be separate or alone.
5. I will never give up hope, because I can always trust in love.

CHAPTER THREE

❖

THE POWER OF ATTITUDES IN HEALTH

*Perhaps true healing
has more to do with
listening with unconditional love
than with trying
to fix people up.*

PAST PERSPECTIVES ON HEALTH

For centuries there has been a tendency for us to think of health only in terms of our physical bodies. Both medical practitioners and patients oftentimes concentrate on the body and focus on physical symptoms. The emphasis in Western medicine has been on physical examination, with diagnosis and treatment being based primarily on that. There was not so much attention given to the subtle spiritual and psychological aspects of a patient's illness.

When I (Jerry) was in medical school, the medical community was quite reluctant to look very seriously at the possibility that our attitudes—the thoughts and feelings we hold in our minds—could play an important role in illness and healing. Throughout the past decade, however, there has been more research, resulting in many scientific papers. There is increasing evidence that there is not an illness known to science that is not affected by our thoughts and feelings and that our attitudes can play a significant role in our ability both to recover from disease and to maintain positive health.

Mostly the physicians of the past were trained to look for the cause of illness in factors such as infection, heredity, trauma, and toxins. Since the 1950s there has been increased interest in how our state of mind and spirit affects our health, either helping to keep us well or making us susceptible to illness.

It is fascinating to note that physicians in general practice have stated that over 50 percent of all the patients they see do *not* have organic illnesses that can be treated by traditional medical techniques. There have been studies showing that over 80 percent of the patients seen by general practitioners would get well without any form of medical intervention.

One medical center, Kaiser Permanente in the San Francisco
Bay Area, reported that the largest portion of their patient
population was what they called the Worried Well—people
who do not have organic disease but are seeking treatment
for symptoms that worry them.

SUSCEPTIBILITY TO ILLNESS

Certainly there are infectious diseases that are clearly caused
by viruses and bacteria. But can there be anything more
infectious than emotions? Our state of mind can play a prime
role in protecting us or helping us recover from illnesses of
this kind. Our bodies' immune systems know how to heal
infections caused by most viruses and bacteria, and they will
do this healing work automatically.

We are now seeing how closely our minds and our immune systems work together, joined as one in the process
of maintaining optimal health. Most of us have had the
experience that when we are feeling good about ourselves
and the world around us, and when we are happy and at
peace with ourselves, we can be around other people who
have infections but we don't pick up their bug.

If you have migraine headaches, diabetes, heart problems,
peptic ulcers, ulcerative colitis, or dermatological conditions,
just to name a few, you have probably noticed that your
state of mind has a lot to do with whether you have symptoms or are feeling perfectly well.

THE POWER OF OUR THOUGHTS IN WELLNESS

I (Jerry) once treated a very successful photographer, whom
I will call Keith. His story contains an important teaching
about the ways that our holding on to the past can have a
very powerful effect on our bodies.

Keith was about forty years of age and had a severe,
chronic constipation problem, which had not responded

well to medical treatment. As we worked together, Keith told me that his father had died about twenty years before and that they had an unhealed relationship. Keith was holding inside himself a lot of anger that he was unable to express.

At his father's funeral Keith had felt numb and there were no tears. Since that time he had not only had a chronic constipation condition but he had also been periodically depressed. His repressed feelings of anger and grief had been affecting his body all this time.

In our sessions together Keith began to express himself and come to grips with the angry thoughts he had kept hidden from himself. He found that these feelings were very human and that he did not have to feel guilty about them. In one session following this discovery he burst out crying, sobbing for more than half an hour over the loss of his father. For nearly twenty years he had denied his grief, holding it in all that time, until he finally found it safe to let it go and experience it.

Keith began to see that he had choices. He chose to no longer hold on to his anger or to bury it in the recesses of his mind. He no longer felt that his anger was serving him in any way, except to keep him bound up and miserable inside. I was fascinated to once again be reminded of how quickly we are able to let go of something when we no longer find value in it.

Keith began to forgive himself and his father. And, yes, the chronic constipation and recurring depression disappeared. As time went on, he began to feel a spiritual connection in his life and found new purpose in helping others. He began to assist others who had difficulty mourning the loss of loved ones from long ago.

The creativity of Keith's photography blossomed. He became a very joyful person who felt that the meaning of his life was to help others and to share his love. He said, "You teach what you want to learn, and I don't know what words can best describe what has happened to me, but I believe I have undergone a deep healing and a spiritual transformation."

RELEASING OURSELVES FROM PAIN

When we are in pain, we often find that the thoughts we hold in our minds can bring us relief and comfort even when medication has not been successful. This has been noted even by people experiencing great hardship, such as with prisoners of war, who found that they could dissociate themselves from painful circumstances through active imagination. Concentrating on happy experiences from their past allowed them to take their minds off their bodies.

When I (Jerry) was in Atlanta, Georgia, several years ago, I remember visiting an eight-year-old boy named Billy who had leukemia. He was a great teacher for me, showing me how we can create thoughts in our minds that can reduce physical pain. The pain medication that doctors had prescribed for Billy did not seem to be working, and he had a lot of pain in his legs.

I asked Billy to tell me about some of his happiest experiences, and he told me that what he liked to do best was to ski and play in the snow. I asked him, "What would happen if you put snow on your legs?" He answered, "My legs would get cold and then they would become numb."

"Do you have a good imagination?" I asked him.

"Yes," he said.

So I asked him to close his eyes. I gave him some *active imagination* suggestions. I had him imagine himself out in the snow playing, putting snow on his legs so that they became numb and he no longer felt any pain. In about five minutes he got a big smile on his face, and he told me that the pain was gone.

ACTIVE IMAGINATION AND EVERYDAY LIFE

Although we may not be consciously aware of it, we all carry around mental pictures every moment of our lives. These pictures can be either positive or negative. When we are feeling a lack of peace, we frequently find that the pictures we are holding in our minds are negative ones, based on fearful experiences from the past. When we are peaceful inside, the pictures we hold in our minds are positive ones, based on experiences from our past when we were doing something pleasurable, perhaps when we were feeling loving toward ourselves and the world around us.

Several years ago I (Jerry) was asked to see a seven-year-old boy, whom I will call Dick. Dick turned out to be a valuable teacher for me about the power of the pictures we hold in our minds and the fact that it is possible to choose those pictures.

Dick had severe asthma. It was so severe that he had to go to the emergency room at his local hospital several times a week for shots. Somehow there didn't seem to be any kind of medication that was very helpful on a continuing basis. When I met Dick, he had not been in school for more than two days in a row for more than a year.

I saw the child separately, as well as with both parents, in order to get a full family history. What I found out was that there was terrible marital discord, with many noisy verbal arguments. I learned that Dick had discovered that there was some "magic" in his having asthma attacks.

Dick had learned how to bring on an asthma attack. During a hot argument between his parents, when they were threatening to divorce each other, Dick would manage to have an asthma attack. And guess what? The parents would abruptly stop arguing and talking about divorce. It was as if Dick had become very powerful, with the ability to make his parents stop fighting.

You don't have to be a psychiatrist to see that this seven-year-old boy had quite a bit to gain from holding on to his illness. And it seemed to me that he was not about to give up that power or let anyone else take it away from him. He was immobilized with fear but with the magic of thinking he could control his parents so that they would do as he wished.

After meditating I decided to take a rather unorthodox approach. Because I believed that Dick was threatened by me as a person who might take his asthma attacks away from him, I took the opposite approach. I told Dick that I knew of a way that he could have even bigger and better asthma attacks, which he could bring on if he ever wanted to scare his parents and get them under his control.

Naturally Dick was pretty surprised by what I said, but I sure got his attention. With great enthusiasm he immediately said, "How?" He was quite eager to know how he could achieve even greater control over his parents.

I told him he could do this by using his active imagination. I could teach him how to do it. I drew a picture of his lungs and bronchi and even molded them out of clay. I told him that by using his imagination he could imagine his bronchi getting smaller and smaller until an asthma attack would occur.

I told Dick that if he wanted to, we could do that right now and I could record his asthma attack on my tape recorder. He wanted to do it right away. Dick had a wonderful imagination and was able to have an attack almost instantly.

While he was gloating about his accomplishment, I went on to say, "You know, someday you might want to go to a party or do something that is fun but your parents won't let you because of your asthma. Would you like me to teach you a way to get rid of an attack by using your imagination?" I received another enthusiastic yes.

That day I taught Dick to use his imagination so that he could increase the size of his bronchi so that he could breathe freely and easily whenever he wished. He thought this was great!

We then began to talk about Dick's fears. I told him that perhaps there was another way of dealing with his fear. I suggested that he might talk to his parents whenever he got scared. I told him it was up to him and that I was not telling him what to do. But I just wanted him to know that he always had choices.

I assured him that I was not going to try to take his asthma away from him. I just wanted him to know that many times he really had a choice to be well or not.

In my professional life I have been impressed by the fact that when people really know they have choices, they more often than not choose what is healthy.

Well, that is exactly what happened with Dick. He experimented for a couple of weeks, as if he had been given a new toy, a new control device. He also learned that he had the ability to control his own thoughts, to share his feelings, and to be honest and direct rather than manipulative.

After about two weeks the number of hospital visits began to lessen. A month later I received a phone call from the teacher saying that Dick was going to school every day, for the first time that school year.

Harry

Children have been some of my most valuable teachers, and this has been especially so in the use of active imagination. One of my teachers was Harry, a four-year-old boy who was referred to me because he continued to have bowel movements in his pants and had never been successfully toilet trained. At the time we met, he had just moved to California from New York, where he and his family had been in psychotherapy for over a year.

When Harry was about a year old, his baby sister was born. Being the baby, she immediately started getting a lot of attention that had once gone to Harry.

I think that most of us have been in situations where if we were not successful in our efforts to get love and positive attention, we would go after negative attention in an effort just to have some kind of attention directed toward us. This usually happens on a subconscious level of course. It certainly felt to me that this might be what was happening in Harry's case.

I was looking for some way to get Harry's attention because, like Dick, it seemed that he was getting a lot out of his symptoms. I started by asking Harry what interested him the most, and his immediate response was "fire engines and spaceships! I want to be the first boy to go to the moon."

I told Harry, "You know, I could help you make that happen by using your imagination. In your imagination I could even make you famous. How would you like to be the first boy to take a shit on the moon?" (I used the word *shit* because I had noted that it was the word both his parents and he used to describe defecation.)

Harry was getting very excited about all this and he asked me how he could do that. I went on to explain that we could go into my bathroom and imagine that it was a space machine. Remembering what he had said about his interest in fire engines and spaceships, I added, "This is a special space machine that has a fire engine on it. And this fire engine is special because it has a toilet on it."

I told Harry that by closing his eyes he could imagine that my toilet was a toilet on the fire engine and the fire engine was on a spaceship. And he could imagine that after he reached the moon, he could shit in the toilet and the next day, in newspapers all over the world, people would read the headlines: HARRY—THE FIRST BOY TO SHIT ON THE MOON!

What I didn't expect on this trip to the moon was that Harry would make himself captain and I would be his first officer. On our ten-minute trip to the moon he gave me a lot of orders. But it was worth enduring because a few minutes after arriving at the moon I heard Harry grunt. This was followed by a plop, plop. Harry smiled with delight, and I yelled, "Eureka!"

After the trip to the moon Harry and I began to talk about his fears of not getting enough love and his anger toward his baby sister. He continued to have bowel movements in his pants for a few weeks, and then he began to go to the bathroom on a regular basis. With his ability to express his fears he gradually came to see that his sister was no longer an enemy.

Over the past few years there have been more and more people writing books and scientific papers to help us understand the important links between the thoughts we hold in our minds and our health. The following is just a sampling of some of the work being done in this area.

PIONEERS IN THE HEALING POWERS OF ATTITUDES

Norman Cousins

Norman Cousins, who died in 1990, dedicated nearly two decades of his life to spreading the word about the important link between our bodies and our minds. For many years he was the publisher of *Saturday Review*. Then, when his doctors told him that he had a rare, life-threatening illness, he became interested in how our thoughts affect our physical wellness. He was close to death, and his physicians told him there was nothing more that they could do for him.

Norman left the hospital determined to get well. He had a movie projector brought to him with a lot of funny movies by the Marx brothers, Charlie Chaplin, Laurel and Hardy, and others. He played these films over and over, for hours and days on end. In the end he got well, and in the process discovered that laughter was indeed "powerful medicine."

So many people in the medical community were impressed by his dramatic recovery that his story was recounted in the *New England Journal of Medicine*. At that time Cousins stated, "We have allies out there, a lot of doctors who believe as we do but need encouragement."

Cousins lived for many years after that, enjoying vibrant health and lecturing to medical groups, as well as nonmedical people, all over the world. His books, *Anatomy of an Illness* and *Head First*, continue to be very helpful to many people. He was a dear friend and did a fund-raising lecture for the Center a few years before his death.

Dr. Dean Ornish

Dr. Dean Ornish's book, entitled *Reversing Heart Disease*, was based on cases where people had recovered from life-threatening heart disease. In the book he describes scientific evidence for the fact that a change in attitudes and lifestyle, along with a program of diet and exercise—all factors that we can choose in our lives—can reverse heart disease and reduce the necessity of difficult and expensive medical procedures such as bypass surgery.

Dr. Richard H. Helfant

Traditional medicine has produced many courageous pioneers of the healing arts. One such person is Dr. Richard Helfant, former director of cardiology at Cedars-Sinai Medical Center in Los Angeles, and author of *Women Take Heart: The Hidden Epidemic* (New York: Putnam, 1992). His list of medical credentials and professional papers is a mile long.

After decades of diagnosing and treating heart ailments, Dr. Helfant concluded that medical treatment alone was dealing primarily with the symptoms of heart disease. For the most part medicine had failed to fully address attitudinal causes and risk reduction.

He made dramatic changes in his own life, choosing to resign from his prestigious position, at the pinnacle of his career, to pursue what he believes to be the way to treat and ultimately reduce the risk of heart disease.

He has committed his time, talents, and energy to opening a center for heart patients. This center will provide a retreat setting. The program will include Attitudinal Healing, spiritual concepts, and lifestyle, along with diet and exercise, as well as incorporating more traditional medical treatments. Dr. Helfant is convinced that changing our attitudes can play a major role in reducing the risk of heart disease.

DOCTOR AND PATIENT

It is our feeling that in the past the relationship between patients and physicians has been a vertical one. The physician has been the authority who directs all aspects of treatment. In one sense the patient frequently ends up being the passive, compliant recipient of whatever the doctor prescribes. In that system, to be a good patient, you become obedient, doing whatever the doctor says, and you don't ask too many questions, because there are a lot of patients waiting.

In this system the physician might very well share his or her findings about your health with another medical person but perhaps might not share the same information with you, the patient.

There is a big shift taking place in the minds of both doctors and patients, and it is being brought about by patients. More and more people are developing the attitude that they want to take more responsibility for their health.

Patients want their physicians to act as consultants and friends, not as a general or as God. These patients want to know all the facts, have access to their own records, and they wish to participate conjointly in decisions that affect their own health. They want to have horizontal communication with their doctors. We have seen many patients who will not continue to see a physician unless there is a commitment to relate in this manner. So the attitudes of patients, in many instances, are changing the way doctors and patients communicate. This frequently results in reduced anxiety and fear for the patient, as well as for the doctor, and patients are thus empowered to take more active roles in the healing process.

ATTITUDINAL HEALING IN PSYCHOTHERAPY

Recently there has been an increased interest in the spiritual dimensions of psychotherapy. The usual routine, back in the 1960s, was to refer patients to pastoral counselors if they wished to discuss anything that sounded religious or spiritual.

In more recent years many therapists and their patients have become interested in dealing with subjects such as the "spiritual emptiness" that so many people feel. Oftentimes patients may actually try to find therapists who include spiritual issues in their psychotherapy. There is increased interest in the *transpersonal psychology* movement, where there is much emphasis on bridging spiritual, mental, and physical concepts.

Dr. Frances Vaughan

Dr. Frances Vaughan is a longtime dear friend. She is a practicing clinical psychologist, past president of the Association for Transpersonal Psychology, and the author of numerous articles and books, including *The Inward Arc, Awakening Intuition,* and *Accept This Gift* (with Dr. Roger Walsh).

When we asked Frances how she incorporated spiritual principles into her practice, she replied, "All my life I have been interested in religion, and I have been most interested in how spiritual and psychological principles can join each other.

"I meditate every day, and I have been influenced by *A Course in Miracles,* Buddhist principles, and many other spiritual teachings. I do not belong to any religious organization, and I consider myself to be an eclectic on a spiritual pathway. All my clients are my teachers, and I learn from each of them.

"It is not uncommon for words like *God* or *Higher Power* to be used in the therapy sessions. I find that the principles of forgiveness are very important in my practice. When we are stuck in guilt and anger, we need to learn to let go and to see no value in blame and condemnation.

"I believe that psychotherapy is the process of letting go of fear and increasing the ability to give and receive love. Psychotherapy involves the healing of the wounds of the past so that we can learn to have meaningful relationships in the present. It involves learning to tell the truth about our experiences.

"In the psychotherapy that I do, patients learn to trust themselves and to tune in to their own inner guidance. Since I incorporate spiritual principles in my own life, as well as in my practice, many of the people preselect themselves and are already on journeys of wanting to explore the spiritual dimensions of their lives."

We asked Frances what advice she might give psychologists who had just finished their training and were going out to begin a practice. She replied, "I would tell them to remember to ask for their own inner guidance, to keep their hearts open, and I would remind them to be open to further learning."

Dr. Seymour Boorstein

Dr. Seymour Boorstein is an associate professor of psychiatry at the University of California Medical Center in San Francisco. He is also a psychoanalyst and has been in practice for over thirty years. On his own spiritual path, he has been involved in Buddhist meditation as well as *A Course in Miracles*.

In response to how he uses spiritual principles in his practice, Dr. Boorstein stated, "First of all, I used these principles on myself. It helps me look at the people I see as my teachers and it helps to prevent burnout. I am more optimistic and I'm more happy as an individual. And I am not nearly as tired at the end of the day."

He told us that he found the forgiveness process to be a very important one in psychotherapy. He even cited an example of what happened for a patient he had been seeing for thirty years, who had been diagnosed as schizophrenic, when the patient became a student of *A Course in Miracles*. Although the illness did not totally disappear, there was marked improvement in his mood and adjustment to life.

Some of Seymour's colleagues have felt that bringing spiritual principles into psychotherapy can interfere with the transference process. This, however, has not been Seymour's experience.

Dr. Roger Walsh

Dr. Roger Walsh is a professor of psychiatry at the University of California in Irvine, California. In addition to his teaching responsibilities Roger has a private practice and is a prolific author. He is most respected by his colleagues and has been voted by psychiatry residents as one of their most important teachers. His books, such as *Staying Alive: The Psychology of Human Survival*, *The Spirit of Shamanism*, and *A Gift of Healing*, with Dr. Frances Vaughan, have been tremendously helpful to thousands of people.

Roger has been on his own spiritual quest for many years and has been a student of *A Course in Miracles* since shortly after it was first published. He stated that he felt the Course was perhaps the most powerful book that he has ever read regarding the psychological and spiritual aspects of psychotherapy. He stated that he sometimes uses principles of the Course in his own therapy. We asked Roger how he used spiritual principles in his practice.

He replied, "I don't discuss spiritual principles with all my patients. It depends if I feel it is appropriate and if I feel the patient is genuinely ready. I feel that my own spiritual journey has allowed me to have greater sensitivity about what is going on moment-to-moment with my patients. I look for ways that patients may be creating suffering by not facing their own existential questions.

"When it is appropriate, we may talk about the destructive value of anger and attack in their lives. Contrasted to the way I was before, I now appreciate the great effectiveness of forgiveness as a tool in healing. I value the benefits of my own meditative process. Perhaps the most important contrast for me is that I am a more happy person, both in and out of the office, and that has to help in the therapeutic situation."

GUILT AND FEAR

Guilt and fear not only play havoc with our emotional lives, they also affect our bodies. Many of us, because we have attachments to guilt and fear, end up unconsciously doing things that attack our bodies.

For example, I (Jerry) used to be tremendously accident-prone. I never used to think much about this, except that I just seemed to have a lot of *bad luck*. This explanation neatly fit into the belief system that I was a victim in the world. When I changed my belief system and began to seek another way of looking at the world, I stopped being accident-prone. I had made a decision that I would no longer look upon myself as a victim. I began to recognize, almost instantly, that I had been playing an active part in creating my many "accidents." No way were they bad luck, as I had previously thought.

When I stopped seeing value in feeling guilty about my past behavior and thoughts, I stopped seeing any need to punish myself. I really believe that there is a part of each of us that says, when we are feeling guilty, "Punish yourself or find someone else to be angry with and punish them." So, in the past, I used to spend an enormous amount of time either punishing myself for the guilt I experienced or punishing others by being provocative or attacking.

HEART AND MIND POWER

When our hearts and minds are joined with only loving thoughts, the most powerful healing force known to humanity is experienced—the healing power of love. We are just beginning to discover the unlimited power of the mind and the heart. Too often we constrict our hearts, fencing them in out of fear that we might be hurt or disappointed. Too often we cut off the connection between our minds and our hearts by filling our minds with attacking thoughts that cause us to deny our many past traumas and fears.

Many of us have minds that are quite undisciplined. It may seem as if we have thousands of thoughts spinning around and pulling us in all sorts of different directions. It can seem as if we have absolutely no control over these thoughts. Our egos would have us believe that our minds are the victims of the events happening outside us.

We can learn that we are the ones who create and direct our thoughts. Meditation and prayer can be very effective ways of doing this, teaching us that we really can take responsibility for the thoughts we put in our minds, creating peace and tranquility. It is *not* circumstances outside us that control what we think and feel, although it can be most difficult to believe this when our minds are busy and confused.

Healing the mind and the heart is an inside job and is the key for creating positive health throughout our lives.

Affirmations
1. Today I will remind myself that health is inner peace and that healing is letting go of fear.
2. I can always choose to experience inner peace regardless of the state of my body.
3. Today I want to experience joy, and I will do this by letting go of all my grievances.
4. By not condemning myself today I will find peace.
5. I am willing today to let go of all my unforgiving thoughts and by so doing I will let go of suffering.

❖

HEALING ATTITUDES IN OUR RELATIONSHIPS

When we truly want to have peaceful relationships,
we will stop telling other people what to do
and we will practice love and forgiveness.

THE PURPOSE OF RELATIONSHIPS

Perhaps the reason we have so many relationship problems is that we do not fully understand their purpose. The solutions to these problems become more clear to us when we realize that the true purpose is for joining. As we will see later in the book, we often try to use relationships to judge each other and make illusions of being separate from one another.

Can there be anything more important in the world than our relationships with other people? Most of us would agree that there is not. And yet, as we go through the day, it is all too easy to focus our attention on *everything but* the ways we relate to each other.

The world is such a busy place that many of us get caught up in the sheer busy-ness of it. Each day we race around at great speeds trying to accomplish all the things we feel we need to accomplish just to survive. At the end of the day, weary and tense, it is hard to believe that what we're feeling might be directly related to the judgments and condemnations we have made concerning other people as well as ourselves.

SEEING BEYOND THE EGO'S EYES

We are often tempted to find in our relationships an opportunity to experience "justified anger" and even rage, and to blame and point the finger of guilt toward others. The goal of relationships then becomes one of finding an enemy, and seeing other people as projections of our own feelings. We are soon using our relationships to hide our own feelings from our awareness, rather than seeing in our relationships an opportunity to experience love. What we describe here are the perceptions of the ego's thought system.

When we are feeling overwhelmed, exhausted, and tense, it is easy to believe everything the ego tells us and to co-operate with it in creating a reality of separation, unfor-giveness, and even all-out war. All too frequently we then use relationships to project our own feelings to other people so that it appears that those others are causing all the horrible things we are experiencing. In this way the real source of our feelings is hidden from our awareness, and we begin to believe the illusions we ourselves have made—that what we think and what we feel is caused by people and events outside us and that we are helpless victims.

We all know how convincing our ego's thoughts can be, making it appear that what we are seeing and feeling really is the only way of looking at the world. At such times we can remind ourselves that we make those thoughts our-selves. They are only a single aspect of us, an aspect wedded only to the physical body. These perceptions can seem to be the only true reality there is—and we become convinced that we must always be on our guard to protect ourselves from the outside world. If fear is the ego's calling card, then guilt, blame, and unforgiveness are its weapons, which it will pull out and use for attacking other people whenever an opportunity arises.

To remind ourselves that there are other ways of looking at relationships than the ones our egos present, we have only to look upon them as reflections of our own fears. When we are crossing a street and we see a huge truck suddenly racing toward us, our internal warning signals send us scrambling for the safety of the curb. Events such as this can be very convincing, especially when the ego claims it is responsible for warning us. It then grasps the incident as proof that it is always right, that the world is a very dan-gerous place and we must always be watching out for people who would hurt us and make us their victims. When we have attachments to those times when we were hurt or in danger, we can easily forget that the ego's formula demands that we leave out our spiritual identity.

The thought system we call the ego can be not only very convincing but also very loud and insistent. We can calm it down momentarily by courteously asking it to "please be quiet for just a second." Usually our egos will give us that second, but not much more. That precious second can be the golden opportunity for reminding ourselves that there is another way of looking at the world. We can choose to look at our fearful ego messages and find our own call for help and love and our own spiritual identity.

Through the eyes of love we find only joining and forgiveness. Through the ego's eyes we can easily find the thoughts, emotions, words, and actions to create separation in all our relationships.

USING WORDS FOR JOINING OR SEPARATION

I (Diane) have long been an advocate of women's issues, particularly as they apply to the inequities that surround our family and work lives. The fact that over 70 percent of the world's work is done by women when only 1 percent of its wealth is owned by them simply understates the reality of the grave inequality that continues to exist worldwide.

Over the years I have found that it is not my cause but the way I choose to express it that can create a chasm instead of a bridge between myself and other people. When I speak on these issues, before groups or in personal conversations, I receive back a wide range of reactions: the excitement of new awareness, sympathy, defensiveness, anger, and attack. Clearly, whenever I interjected anger, blame, and attack into my own statements, similar reactions were immediately forthcoming from those around me. However, when I stated the facts along with creating a safe environment, one where dialogue could take place to work toward positive solutions, the relationships we established were very different. They became enthusiastic and creative, leading to higher levels of awareness.

Our egos often find opportunities in relationships to prove to the world that "I am right and you are wrong." The ego can use any knowledge we have for this, drawing references from the fields of philosophy, religion, culture, psychology, gender issues, or any other field to "prove" that we are better than another person. There is no end to the stockpiles of ammunition we can find to create separation between people.

Our egos see relationships as something to be used. For example, one man told us that he felt that relationships were like cars: "You go out and get a new one, enjoy it for a while, and then when it starts breaking down, you just go out and replace it by buying a new one."

We agreed that this was certainly one way of looking at relationships. But we also suggested that maybe it was possible that if a person kept having his car break down one after another, just maybe it was the driver that needed fixing, not the cars.

Perhaps that man's comments are not all that unusual in our society. In the throwaway world we live in, where we are encouraged just to buy a new one instead of fixing the old, it's no wonder that we might treat many people in our lives the same way.

A Spiritual Perspective

Our spiritual selves see our relationships as providing opportunities for joining and acceptance, as opposed to separation and judgment. Through this spiritual vision, relationships are seen as opportunities to see each other as extensions and mirrors of each other.

From a spiritual viewpoint, relationships can be seen as laboratories of life where we discover what unconditional love is really all about. The purpose of relationships is seen as an opportunity to learn how to heal the illusion of separation and to experience all hearts and minds as one. In this laboratory of life we discover how to transform fear, guilt, and blame into love.

WHY SOME RELATIONSHIPS DON'T SEEM TO WORK

Fear

Simply put, the main reason relationships fail or become difficult in our lives is our attachment to fear. Fear, blame, and guilt play a main role in sabotaging any hope of experiencing love or intimacy, since they block our awareness of love's presence just as putting up a huge wall would block our view of an awe-inspiring landscape. Each of these in its own way creates a barrier, and although the form may be slightly different in each case, the end result is always the same.

Whether it is fear, blame, or guilt, each emanates from the deeply felt belief that we don't truly believe that we deserve to be happy. Therefore we certainly can't allow ourselves to have intimate, trusting, and nourishing relationships because they would probably make us happy. While part of us knows that love is our true state, we often remain fearful, ensuring that we will seek but never find what we are looking for.

Here is a list, based on fear, of some common reasons why it can seem impossible to have harmonious, growing, loving relationships:

- We cannot trust love.
- We cannot trust people.
- We are only going to be victimized.
- Our past hurtful experiences will only be repeated.
- We will be abandoned.
- The other person will refuse to do what we want them to.
- We will be giving other people, including our parents, the power to decide whether or not we are lovable.
- Our loved ones will die and leave us alone and lonely, proving that nothing is lasting, especially love.

- People will do things that are unforgivable.
- When we are in relationships, we make it possible for other people to hurt us.

Fear of Intimacy

To some people the word *intimacy* can be frightening. Remember that another way of spelling that word is IN-TO-ME-SEE. It is almost impossible to have good relationships with family members, friends, or anyone else when we are afraid not only of love but of intimacy as well. We want to be able to share our deepest, innermost spiritual self with others, yet we guard against this possibility, believing it is necessary to protect our vulnerability.

The Role of the Past and the Future

Our attachments to the past and the future keep our fears of intimacy and love alive. Even when our past relationships have been quite grim, we use them to predict what will happen in the future.

We may be able to look around us and see that it really is possible to have more loving relationships, but we still hold on to the past as if it was the only way. Why? Because we feel that by doing this we can control what will happen to us; and we believe this illusion of control will keep us safe.

Grim memories of past unsuccessful relationships discourage us from opening ourselves up to the present, with its unpredictable, seemingly uncontrollable possibilities. Fearing that history will repeat itself in the future, we recreate the past, making it impossible for us to live fully in the present.

It's Your Fault That I Am Not Happy

So many of us go through life believing that things would be a lot better, and we would be a lot happier, if the other person in the relationship would either disappear or change. Then things would be different. The world's law states,

"When something goes wrong, find someone else to blame." Are you familiar with that law? And is anyone truly made happier because they live by that law?

When we find ourselves unhappy or in distress, we start following that law almost as if our very lives depended on it. We start looking outside ourselves, beyond our own boundaries, for someone or something that is the "cause" of our woes, and as we do this, we may become convinced that our unhappiness is the "effect" of other people's deeds. We begin feeling victimized by the world, or at least by the people in our present or past relationships.

To heal our relationships we need to explore the often unpleasant and hurtful experiences we have had in the past in order to determine where we are suffering, from what, and why. As we look at the past, it is important to avoid the quagmire of questions such as who did what to whom, which is only pursuing the road of blame rather than the road of love.

To lift ourselves from the quagmire of feeling like victims of what others have done to us in the past, we need to stop seeking to attach guilt or blame to ourselves or others. This does not mean, however, denying that we or other people have done things that may have been less than loving, for indeed such things have occurred.

It is important to have a full awareness of what has or hasn't occurred in our past. (There are many positive methods of therapy and numerous well-trained therapists to help, if needed, with this experience.) We must first find within ourselves a willingness to forgive the past, to no longer seek justification for our pain in the actions of others. It is then that we can move forward into new relationships, living fully in the present. If we continue to play the victim role, we will not be able to move off the track of helplessness and onto the road of self-empowerment.

When we stop trying to justify the suffering we have experienced by seeking other people or situations to blame, we unhook ourselves from the painful past. We begin to see that it is possible to take responsibility for the thoughts and feelings we put in our minds. And we begin to experience ourselves in a new way, not as helpless victims but as people on the road to self-empowerment.

WE ARE NEVER UPSET FOR THE REASONS WE THINK[1]

A number of years ago we met a man (I'll call him Richard) who was quite successful in the world, very learned and accomplished. He was also extremely chauvinistic and domineering.

While Jerry and I both recognized that Richard expressed these attitudes, our reactions to him were very different. Throughout any visit we had with him I became very combative, and by the time we were ready to go our separate ways, I was ready to pound him. Jerry, however, saw Richard as fearful and defensive, responding to him as if he was giving a call of help for love. Jerry was always very honest, loving, and compassionate with Richard.

After we went through the same scenario several times, I felt that I really needed to explore the roots of my dilemma. Intellectually I was aware of the value of responding to Richard's behavior in a compassionate and loving way. But try as I might, I could barely muster a few crumbs of tolerance— and I mean only a few! *Agitation, anger,* and even *violence* are words that would best characterize my true feelings toward him.

Only by taking another look at the past for the purpose of healing the present was I able to release myself and find another way of looking at my relationship with Richard.

MY PROJECTION OF MY FATHER ONTO OTHERS

As I honestly looked at my own feelings, it became increasingly clear to me that domineering behavior was a painful reminder of my relationship with my father.

Although I had done much inner work to heal my relationship with my dad, I had never allowed myself to fully experience the anger and agitation I felt toward him in response to his domineering personality. When I did so, I was shocked to discover what came up. My self-image as a "good girl," someone who was always nice and sweet, was suddenly overruled by violent feelings around anger that I had never released. Once again I heard that little voice within reminding me, "When the student is ready, the teacher will appear." So who had shown up in my life but the perfect teacher, one whose outward behavior provided the catalyst for igniting the rage I still held inside me.

My violent reaction to this "teacher" had its roots in my own mind, projected onto him by my perceptions of my father as domineering and controlling. In my deep-seated willingness and desire to heal my past, I had created a new relationship where there was an opportunity to complete my unfinished business with my father.

Although I was still angry with my father, I could see that I was mostly angry at myself for allowing him to dominate and control me when I was a child. Having never stood up to him—either as a child or as a young woman—I was now experiencing heightened awareness of this new opportunity to stand up to Richard.

Finally I saw the path I had to take to let go of my perceptions about my father and the ways I had chosen to respond to him in the past. I was able to experience myself in a new way, forgiving and letting go of my painful memories that had been created as much by my own reactions as by my father's actions. I let go of my blame, no longer judging either of us, and began to see another way of looking at relationships where these themes of chauvinism and control were expressed. I then discovered that I had many more choices and that the only limitations were the ones I placed on myself.

My relationship with Richard changed instantly, and I was able to see the call for help in his behavior for the first time. My own response to him then became clear, caring, and even compassionate.

I no longer felt like a victim. I was able to separate my own previous experiences from the present ones I was having with Richard. Interestingly enough, when I realized this,

I experienced Richard in an entirely new way. I now feel exceedingly grateful to him for providing me with the catalyst that allowed me to complete more unfinished business I had with my father.

The process of healing relationships is truly like the opening of a lotus blossom, unfolding in layers upon itself, gradually revealing more and more of the beauty within.

EACH ENCOUNTER IS A RELATIONSHIP

Each and every encounter, with every person we meet, whether for a fleeting moment or an extended period of time, constitutes a relationship. Whether it's a family member or a chance meeting on the street, a person whose services we are employing, a person who is employing our services, an old friend, a professional acquaintance, a clerk in a store, or a telephone operator—each encounter is an opportunity to choose once again how we are going to relate to others.

Life offers us a constant flow of opportunities for discovering and working out the areas of growth necessary for our own transformation and evolution.

We can segment and compartmentalize our lives, separating the ways we relate according to whether it is business, family matters, sports, education, or making purchases in the store. But no matter what the activity that brings us together, we affect each other according to how we choose to relate.

We have relationships throughout every aspect of our lives, even when we are alone, for it is then that we have to relate to ourselves and with the environment around us.

RELATIONSHIPS WITH THE ENVIRONMENT AND WITH ANIMALS

When looking at the subject of relationships, it can be easy to forget that it is our relationships not just with other humans but also with other creatures and the earth itself that are important. In recent years there has been a wake-up call going on around the world, a small voice at first, but one that is now getting louder and louder.

It is as if most of us have been asleep, and in our sleep we have been destroying the environment. The rain forests and the ozone layer are disappearing. In many ways we have been relating to the earth in anything but loving ways. We have not been responsible, either as individuals or as companies, in protecting the planet and all the forms of life that make it the wonderful place it is. We have polluted the water and the air. And authorities tell us that if we don't do something about it immediately, it may be too late.

We have yet to meet a person who trashes out his or her environment who doesn't also trash out his or her relationships. When we begin to see that it is our responsibility to love all that is life, all that is living, we then begin to make a difference in expressing our love to all the animals, trees, and all of nature that makes up our environment.

It becomes important to see the world as our friend and not our enemy. By loving the planet, we then begin to do our part in cleaning it up and keeping it in its natural, healthy, beautiful state. Over 150 years ago, Chief Seattle addressed Congress with a message that we think is equally important today. In it he said,

> This we know. The earth does not belong to man; man belongs to the earth. This we know. All things are connected like blood which unites one family. All things are connected.
> Whatever befalls the earth befalls the sons of the earth. Man did not weave the web of life; he is merely a strand in it. Whatever he does to the web, he does to himself.

The same principles that help us to learn how to be more loving in our relationships with other people are equally valuable in healing our relationships with the earth and all its creatures. What comes to mind at this moment is a story that our friends Trenje and Paul Horn shared with us while we were in Victoria, B.C., lecturing.

About a year before our visit with them someone had brought Trenje a baby lamb that was dying. The lamb was deaf and blind, and it could not walk because it hadn't seen that it was even supposed to. Well, Trenje is an Earth Mother who loves the earth and all that lives on it. She especially loves to care for old, sick farm animals that no one else wants. Her magic medicine of course is love.

Trenje and Paul took this lamb into their house and bottle-fed it, making it a part of the family. They cared for this lamb with the same care they would give a human baby. They even went so far as to take it to bed with them to keep it warm. They helped it learn to walk, although it was still blind and deaf. And far from being the poor defenseless creature it had once seemed to be, it became quite healthy and strong.

This most affectionate lamb demonstrated the power and the miracle of love. You see, even the blindness and deafness eventually disappeared.

MIRRORING OURSELVES

One of the most confusing aspects of any relationship is the discomfort we experience just being in the presence of certain people. No matter what they do or say, there is something about them that evokes in us a response that is heavily tainted with repugnance, combativeness, anger—anything but acceptance or love.

Why is it that some people affect us in these ways while with most other people in our lives we feel that we are able to be quite comfortable, loving, and open? Why do we respond so negatively in some people's presence? Is it them? Is it us? Or is it a little of both?

One of the most difficult realities perhaps any of us has to face is the fact that *what I dislike or cannot tolerate in other people is the personality trait that I still haven't come to terms with in my own life.* Whatever is bothering me about the other person mirrors something that I have not forgiven either in myself or in someone from my past. My intolerance in my present relationships is ultimately an intolerance for myself or someone from my past. For example, let's say you become very upset by a person who has a very domineering attitude in the workplace. Though you're upset, you do not seem to be able to change the way you feel when you're around him. Then, one day, you realize that this person reminds you of your father, whose domineering ways frightened you when you were a child.

How can this be? It happens because we store all our past experiences—both the loving and the hurtful ones—back in the recesses of our minds. Most of the time we're hardly aware of the memories of these experiences being there, and it is difficult to believe that our pasts really could affect the way we view our worlds in the present.

When another person offers an opinion, expresses a thought, or reflects a feeling similar to experiences in our mental storage banks, the past can be called forth, stimulating our old grievances, self-condemnations, or feelings of helplessness. Our knee-jerk reactions to people or situations in the present, then, are really reactions to our past.

Our most difficult relationships often hold up mirrors to us, reflecting back unfinished business from the past. It is only when we are able to take a moment, go into ourselves, and then relive those experiences that we can begin to forgive ourselves or others. To have whole and equal relationships in the present, it is necessary to heal our old, unhealed relationships with ourselves and others from the past.

CONFLICT

How can we find peace of mind when someone else is doing or saying something that is contrary to our wishes? Do we have to behave like a passive amoeba and do we have to give up the values we believe in so that we can avoid conflict in the search for a peaceful existence? Certainly not. But this is perhaps the most widespread misperception about choosing peace over conflict, choosing love over fear. It is the misperception that choosing peace is a sign of weakness and choosing conflict is a sign of strength.

With a deep sense of appreciation we recall the lessons of Mahatma Gandhi. When he was asked to stand up to the British laws of oppression with a show of force and violence against a group of British officers, his response was to choose peace instead of conflict, but to do so as a show of strength and conviction to his ideals. He stated that there were causes for which he was willing to die, and indeed this was one of them. But there was no cause anywhere for which he was willing to take another's life. He demonstrated to the whole world that his greatest strength was not physical, not in his muscles or in his armaments, but simply in the attitudes he held about his beliefs.

Gandhi believed that the strength of our deepest convictions can best be expressed through nonviolent action. By expressing ourselves peacefully we not only communicate our deepest convictions but we uphold the ultimate values of human dignity. He believed that in this way we can disarm even the most aggressive blows of physical coercion and show that force is ineffective, outdated, and pathetically shameful. He was most successful, as history has shown.

MY THOUGHTS ARE MY RESPONSIBILITY

Attitudinal Healing reminds us that it is ultimately not other people or events in the world that make us upset. Rather it is our thoughts, attitudes, and judgments about these people or events, as well as how they trigger our own feelings from the past, that causes our distress in the present.

We begin to see from this that it is not other people or events that need to change in order for us to be happy. Rather, we can direct our own lives and no longer be victims by recognizing that we have alternatives about how we approach our problems. We can choose what we put into our own minds, how we interpret the world, and how we respond to it.

We can recognize that each relationship we have in our lives, regardless of the form, can be healthy and whole on the inside if we give up our idea of what it should look like on the outside. It literally takes tearing up the mental scripts that we have for others that portray the way we think they should be in order for them to be happy. In reality our scripts for others are only written to make us feel safe.

It is the realization that, without exception, each of us, precisely through our relationships, even the seemingly negative ones, acts as a powerful teacher to the other.

LEARNING FROM OUR ENEMIES

A few years ago, at the University of California campus in Santa Barbara, we had the wonderful experience of working on a documentary film with His Holiness the Dalai Lama. In one segment he was interviewed by a group of children, ages six to sixteen.

A fifteen-year-old girl asked the Dalai Lama if he would tell them about his most powerful teacher. He turned to the two of us (Diane and Jerry) and said, with a grin, "This answer may surprise you both." Then he turned back to the children and said, "Although I have had many brilliant and inspiring influences in my life, I have to say that my very strongest teacher, without a doubt, was Chairman Mao. Because of our opposing views on the future of Tibet, many hardships were experienced over a period of many years. If it wasn't for Mao, I would not have been able to have the opportunity to truly learn about tolerance and forgiveness." To us this was truly an example of a healed attitude.

If you really stop to think about it, however, wouldn't you agree that it has been through the hardest experiences and the most difficult people in your life that you have learned the most? It is so hard to admit that the seemingly most adverse circumstances of our lives frequently present us with the most profound learning experiences.

It is when we fully *embrace* these difficult situations that we begin to see their connections with positive changes that truly helped to make our lives more meaningful. Our acceptance and gratitude for these lessons ultimately liberates us, becoming the source of complete forgiveness that sets us free from all our past grievances.

In our own lives, and in the lives of so many people we have had the great privilege of meeting, it has been demonstrated again and again that reaching this plateau literally turns our lives around. Some of the most adverse circumstances and challenging relationships have become pivotal points from which we have discovered new strengths, qualities, and inspirations. We can sincerely and honestly say that our less-than-perfect lives, filled with far less than perfect relationships, have actually turned out to be *absolutely perfect* because they acted as catalysts, giving us opportunities for learning the greatest lessons.

As we begin to see relationships in this new light, we feel ourselves rise from the quagmire of confusion. We begin to see our lives not in fragments but as a whole. With this sense of wholeness comes the perspective that each and every person and experience in our lives, without exception, is ultimately a positive opportunity, providing an empowering lesson.

HEALING IS A UNILATERAL CHOICE

Healing our relationships is ultimately our own choice, since it isn't really the other person we are actually forgiving. It is only our own attitudes and judgments about them that need to be forgiven.

It is our thoughts and judgments today, and no longer the other person, that cause us pain in the present. And since these thoughts and judgments are ours and ours alone, it is we who need to commit ourselves to the act of forgiveness, to change our minds and release ourselves from past grievances. It is ultimately our relationship with ourselves that needs to be healed, and it is only we who can do that, if we choose.

Is It Possible to Heal All Our Relationships?

Yes! It is possible to heal not just some but all our relationships. We can do this by giving up any preconceived form or mental scripts we may have written about others. We can do it by having a willingness to remove all grievances and attack thoughts from our minds. And we can do this through the process of forgiveness. We can do this by

- *Recognizing* that we are *not victims* of our relationships but full *participants* in them
- *Taking responsibility* for our own thoughts, our own choices, and our own emotions, and *not blaming* the other person for what has happened in the relationship
- *Choosing to see* others as *loving* us or, if we perceive them as attacking us, choosing to see them as *fearful* and giving a call of help for love
- *Remembering* that *what we perceive* in others, and in the outside world, is a *projection* of the thoughts—either positive or negative—in our own minds
- *Learning to love* ourselves and others by forgiving rather than judging
- *Becoming "love finders"* rather than "fault finders"
- *Directing ourselves* and choosing *to be peaceful* inside, regardless of what is happening outside us

These realizations can literally affect every aspect of our lives. We can begin to look anew at the world and all our relationships in it. We can begin to recognize that the healing of our relationships is directly related to healing the attitudes we are holding in our minds about those relationships.

Affirmations

1. I choose to heal my relationship with *myself* by letting go of my self-condemnation.
2. I choose to join with others, instead of separating myself from them, by letting go of my judgments of them.
3. I choose to tear up all the scripts that I have for the way I think people should be in my life.
4. I choose to remember that it is not *how much* I do or say that ultimately counts in my relationships but *how much love* I do or say it with.
5. The words I choose in my communications always determine whether my intentions are for joining or for separating.
6. It is ultimately through my relationships that I will experience unconditional love.
7. Today I choose to remember that I do deserve the right to be happy.
8. Today I choose to give up feeling like a victim of my relationships and I will take responsibility for my life.
9. Whenever I get caught in the past or the future, I will choose to remember that love can only be experienced in the present.
10. I can choose love instead of fear in all my relationships.

PART II

❖

CHANGE YOUR LIFE

CHAPTER FIVE

❖

TEACH ONLY LOVE—THE GOLDEN RULE OF PARENTING

*Newborn infants are magnificent
teachers of unconditional love
because they make no judgments
on their parents, accepting them
perfectly, just as they are.*

Newborns as Teachers of Love

At the Center so many of our greatest lessons come from the children themselves. We were reminded of this once again while we were lecturing in New Jersey and heard the following true story, which went directly to our hearts. A young couple had just brought home their newborn infant. It was a Sunday afternoon, and their three-year-old daughter became quite insistent about wanting to go into the baby's room all by herself.

The parents were a little taken aback by the intensity of the little girl's request. They sensed something very urgent and vital in the plea, something that was coming from deep within her. At first they suspected sibling rivalry might be the girl's motivation and, feeling somewhat protective, they were concerned that she might harm the baby. The parents talked it over between them and decided that since they had an intercom between their room and the baby's, they could listen in to make certain that everything was all right.

The little girl tiptoed into the baby's room alone as the parents listened in. They heard their daughter close the door and then listened as her footsteps approached the crib. There was a moment of quiet, and then they heard their daughter's voice softly whisper to the baby: "Baby, remind me what God is like. I am beginning to forget."

Perhaps one of the biggest challenges all of us have is to remember God. We believe that we have much to learn from newborns about the power of unconditional love and that this is one of the things they are here to teach us, if we are only willing to learn from someone so young. We can learn that everyone is our teacher, regardless of her or his age.

We have seen people in deep depression, others in severe physical pain, and even those who are worried about dying, completely change their mood when they hold an infant in their arms. It is very difficult not to smile and feel joy with that very special experience of holding a newborn. All our attention is immediately focused on that miracle of love that we are holding. For that one second, attention to our own body seems to disappear, and we experience something that seems to go beyond ourselves.

Once when we were in Italy with Mother Teresa, she told us of a remarkable woman whom she greatly admired. The woman, who lived in South America, gave her newborn infant the legal name Professor of Love. The name was a gentle reminder to her that every time she was with the child, or even thought about him, she would remember that he was there to teach her about unconditional love. We will never forget this story because it tells so much about childrearing.

We like to think that some of the teachings of unconditional love that newborn infants give their parents are the following:

- They don't care whether you are tall or short, thin or fat; they don't care about the color of your skin, your religious affiliation, or even if you have no religion. They love you unconditionally.
- The power of unconditional love lies in their innocence.
- They don't know about yesterday or tomorrow or what time it is, but they believe that this instant is the only time there is, this instant is a time for love.
- A part of them recognizes that they are spiritual beings—they light up the room wherever they are with the very special light of love that they are. They know that they are the light of the world.
- They don't need words to communicate because a part of them knows that the highest form of communication in this world is the heart-to-heart communication of love, which always takes place without words.
- They teach parents to have patience that they did not

know they possessed, and that infinite patience is an integral part of unconditional love.

- They teach parents the power of gentleness and tenderness.

- They teach parents that our minds are always joined and that we can sense what is going on in each other without even being in the same room.

- They know within their hearts that when you send love, it is always received, and that giving is receiving.

As parents we can learn to see the reflection of ourselves in our children. We believe that almost anyone who has experienced holding a newborn in his or her arms has experienced a power of love that is beyond intellectual understanding.

Whether we describe it as the mystery of life or the miracle of love does not matter. What does matter is that we see children as our most treasured teachers of love and teachers of peace. By reflecting and mirroring their unconditional love we can learn to go beyond the daily frustrations that can occur for each of us during our journey of parenting.

TEACH ONLY LOVE

Two of the happiest and most heroic parents we have ever met, Margie and Ed, have been legal guardians for twenty children, fourteen of them living in the house at one time; six of them were Margie and Ed's own children.

You would think that this would be the world's most chaotic home and a disciplinarian's nightmare, but it is quite the contrary. It is undoubtedly one of the happiest, best-managed households we have ever visited. Each member of the family functions not only independently but for the good of all.

We interviewed them for this book because we wanted to ask them about the trials and tribulations of raising such a large family. We wanted to hear any advice they might offer other parents. Margie and Ed feel that happy parenthood begins with both parents taking care of themselves individually, apart from their identities as parents, and also taking care of their relationship to each other as a couple. Time away from the children, even if it's only a few hours each week, ensures the healthy, independent functioning of the parents within the family unit. In this way they provide models for the children, giving them not only a nest where they can feel safe but visions of themselves as one day sprouting wings, just like their parents, and leaving that nest.

Margie shared a story that helped her look at herself in a new way. One day, during a large gathering of friends and family members at their home, she kept noticing one of her sons, Mark, getting into things. She called him over and said to him, "Mark, it seems like every time I turn around, you're getting into something. What's the deal?" Without so much as batting an eye he replied, "Well, Mom, maybe you're turning around too much!" In this instant Margie was reminded of how important it was to look at the whole of life, not just the fragments that are our own narrow perceptions.

We asked Margie, currently a congresswoman from the state of Pennsylvania, to describe for us something about her goals as a parent. She replied, "We are committed to giving the children, some of whom come from Vietnam and Korea, the best gift we know. That is the gift of SELF-LOVE. We are constantly letting them know how wonderful they are.

"When their behavior needs to be corrected, we readily let them know that we think *they are wonderful but their actions are not!* Invariably they choose to raise their behavior to the level of esteem that we consistently hold out to them, which is 'wonderful.'

Margie and Ed believe that as parents we should let our children know that we ourselves are not perfect. We have pain, depression, frustration, and anger just as they do. They encourage all of us to not be afraid to admit to our children that we are sometimes wrong and to apologize. It's a lot easier for younger members to feel a part of the family when they know that the older members are human too. Teaching only love is a way of life for Ed and Margie. They remind us, once again, to be as consistent as we can in demonstrating and teaching trust, honesty, clarity, tolerance, gentleness, joy, defenselessness, generosity, patience, faith, and open-mindedness. They remind us to seek harmony in what we think, say, and do, both in our own lives and in raising our children, and to listen, really listen, with our full attention.

Margie and Ed's example reminds us of how important it is in parenting not to hide any secrets from ourselves or others and to allow ourselves to be vulnerable. Good parenting is to make forgiveness and love as important as breathing. It is a willingness to admit and share your mistakes with others. It is a willingness to see only the light of love in one another. It is to accept our own lack of perfection and honor our own humanity. It is not to be afraid of love or of being hurt. It is knowing that giving love is the most important thing you can do. And it is, as Mother Teresa has said, "When you give the gift of love, there are no small or large gifts. All gifts of love are the same."

DO WE TEACH LOVE OR FEAR?

There is so much fear around us in the world, and we get exposed to that fear at a very early age. We are living in a world where there is much conflict, aggression, injustice, inequality, and ruthless competition. It is a world where the message has often been, "Get all that you can. Take care of yourself first because it's a *me first* society. Above all, learn how to *do unto others before they do unto you*, or you're just going to turn out to be a loser."

We are often given the message, by our public officials as well as by celebrities, that "dishonesty is not a sin, only getting caught is." We can all point to injustices in our world in which if you have enough money, a good attorney, and you happen to be from the right racial background, you can get away with no prison time and only a light fine when you do get caught.

Often without our being conscious of it, we displace much of our fear and anger, projecting it onto our children. We become impatient, or we lie and deceive. We are only recently discovering how high the presence of emotional, physical, social, and sexual abuse is in our society.

Attitudinal Healing teaches us that we can choose the thoughts we put in our minds and that each of us can learn to pause for a moment, go inside ourselves, and get in touch with the love that is within each of us. It is a love that can be renewed in our hearts and our minds through the lessons our children teach us from the moment they come into our lives.

THE CLASSROOM OF PARENTHOOD

There is no classroom quite like parenting. It enables us— sometimes voluntarily, sometimes involuntarily—to ride a crest of highs and lows as rugged as the Rocky Mountain range itself. Our roles as parents force us to explore areas of our lives that are truly uncharted and to confront them in ways that are decisive and accountable. Our dear friend Robert Young (of the *Father Knows Best* and *Marcus Welby* television programs) and his wife, Betty, told their young daughter one day, "You didn't come into our lives with an instruction manual—and we're doing the very best job we know how!"

Although there are many books on the subject, like Robert and Betty Young we have yet to read a book that tells it all about parenting. For most of us the only teachers we ever had were our own parents when we were children. And many of us have had experiences with our parents we didn't like, and may have wished that our parents had in some ways been different.

It sometimes helps us to ask, Where did our own parents

learn their parenting skills? Why, from their parents of course. If we were able to go back in time and perhaps experience our parents' childhoods through their eyes, we would more easily recognize the source of their parenting skills or lack of them. We might also be more forgiving of their errors in raising us. By and large most of us really do our best when it comes to parenting, with our sense of what's best usually being something we have learned, or not learned, when we ourselves were small children.

Unfortunately when we have not healed our relationships with our parents, we tend to repeat with our own children the very things we objected to when we were children. Find someone who beats up her children and you will probably find someone who was beaten as a child by her own parents. Attitudinal Healing teaches us that we do have a choice about stopping this cycle.

STOPPING THE VICIOUS CYCLE OF GENERATIONAL DYSFUNCTION

Many of us who have been raised in other than perfect environments have heard ourselves say, "I'll *never* treat *my* kids the way my parents treated me!" And then comes the pain of realizing that we are doing exactly that, treating our own children in ways that we swore we never would.

We can also identify with the pain of realizing, at times, that we are doing to our own children *exactly* what we hated our parents doing to us. There is a point of insanity that lurks beneath the surface at these moments, leaving us confused, despondent, and frustrated, feeling helpless and alone as we ask ourselves, If I love my children so much, how could I behave in this way toward them? I, above all people, should know better!

But is knowing better enough? Could it be that our need to create better relationships with our children is directly related to our need for healing our relationships with our parents?

Our pathology in our parental relationships is often dictated by our painfully deep need and desire to bond with them, no matter what the outer form of that relationship might currently take.

For example, a man whom we both know to be quite gentle, insightful, compassionate, and kind with most everyone he knows, had particular problems relating to his son, from the time the boy was quite young until late in his teens. Being a believer in nonviolence, this father would talk things out with his child, but more often than not his temper would flare up, and the discussion would end up in a violent confrontation. He often shook the boy or even struck him, much to his own horror.

The father would feel terrible afterward. But he always somehow justified his actions by saying that his own father had taught him in much the same way, that this had been his father's way of showing his love. Therefore his actions were showing his son that he was cared for and loved.

Even when we are absolutely sure that our parents' actions against us were inappropriate, our minds will oftentimes find ways to somehow make them "right," in order to find a way to bond with them. *We want their approval and love so much that we are willing to join them in their insanity to get it.*

STEPS FOR BREAKING GENERATIONAL CHAINS

There are six important steps we can each take to break the patterns of unhealthy behavior that are passed from one generation to another. They are the following:

1. *Discovery.* Learn to recognize patterns in our own behavior with our children that mirrors behavior we experienced as children.

2. *Exploration.* Seek to understand the motivations behind these patterns—whether we are attempting to create separation or joining.

3. *Bring up old emotions.* Allow ourselves to once again remember and relive emotions such as pain, anger, and fear that were prevalent in our own childhood.

4. *Expression.* Communicate what we are feeling in an environment that is safe for us as well as for others.

5. *Recognize new choices.* Realize that as adults we can now heal the inner child who experienced this pain, anger, and fear.

6. *Choose once again.* Put into action those choices that truly reflect who we are today rather than echoing our parents' feelings and behavior.

THE BIGGEST OBSTACLE TO GOOD PARENTING

In three words, the biggest obstacle to being good parents is: NOT LOVING OURSELVES. Learning to love ourselves isn't just a matter of willpower or saying affirmations, though both of these may play important parts. We truly learn to love ourselves by finishing unfinished business with our own parents. Doing this personal work may take on many forms and is based on being absolutely honest with ourselves about how we feel toward them as parents. As we work with our own behavior patterns, we can begin to have a willingness to forgive them. It also means having a willingness to forgive ourselves for our own perceptions of them, as well as for our own mistakes. We need to "demystify our parents," as John Bradshaw says, in order for us to deal with them on a human level.

If we hope to heal the attitudes we have about raising our own children, we must look at the judgments and beliefs we still hold about the ways our parents raised us. It is helpful to look inside our hearts and be honest with ourselves about what we are feeling toward our parents—the ways they raised us and our feelings toward them.

It is imperative that we honor our humanness and experience our anger and resentment if that is what we discover inside. We need to find a safe, therapeutic way to discover what is truly going on subconsciously in order to consciously make new choices to remove the blocks to our experience of peace and love in our own lives.

If we feel that we did not get approval or love, we need to know that this wasn't because we were unlovable. In my own life I (Jerry) had not resolved feelings I had toward my parents when my children were young. My parents had always expected me to be a good student, which, due to my dyslexia, I definitely was not. As a result I felt a lot of pressure and resentment toward them for pushing me in school. I consequently put a lot of pressure on my two sons to be academic achievers. I sent them a lot of messages based on conditional love: "I will love you more if you get good grades on your report cards, if you keep your room clean, and if you do things that I was not able to do for myself when I was your age."

Fear easily creates a vicious circle, and there is then a great temptation to repeat the same errors. Because of our own unresolved conflicts, we too often end up teaching and demonstrating fear rather than love to our children.

Every time we express conditional love to someone, or they express it to us, we are putting across the message that they are not lovable as they presently are. They would be more lovable if they just learned to do things the way we think they should.

I am grateful, almost beyond words, that my sons, who are now adults with children of their own, have forgiven me. And I am grateful that I have forgiven myself and my parents.

The greatest lesson any of us has to teach each other, and this is especially true in our relationships with our children and our own parents, is to teach only love. But we can teach this only when we are able to accept and love ourselves. You can't really give love until you have experienced it within yourself.

DO AS I SAY, NOT AS I DO!

Is there one among us who hasn't experienced a parent or authority figure in our childhood who has directed us to act one way while they act in exactly the opposite way? "Alcohol and drugs are bad for you," the parent admonishes while sipping evening cocktails and puffing on a cigarette. Or, we hear our parents talking very lovingly and compassionately with an acquaintance, only to overhear them a while later gossiping with someone else about that same person in a way that is quite degrading.

Much of the confusion we have in our own lives, and much of the confusion we pass on to our children, is the result of putting out very mixed messages. How can we expect our children to be honest when we cheat on our income taxes and tell "little white lies" to manipulate and control other people? How can we expect our children to listen to us if we don't really hear what they are trying to say? What kinds of messages do we give our kids when we ask them to do as we say, not as we do? We can only teach honesty by demonstrating honesty and integrity consistently in all our actions.

Unlike the Western Union delivery person whose only responsibility is to see that the message gets to the proper address, we need to actually deliver, accept, and live the message of love in our everyday lives in order to impart it to our children. We need to stay present, to offer our children ourselves as models for listening and receiving, not just deliverers.

Parenting occurs at many levels, since it involves our relationships with our own children, our parents, and ultimately ourselves. In order to heal the attitudes we are teaching to our children, or the attitudes our parents taught us, we must first heal our relationships with ourselves. We do this by forgiving all misperceptions we have about who we are and why we do things.

HEALING THE SPLIT MIND: LEARNING TO BE CONSISTENT IN THOUGHT, WORD, AND DEED

Consistency in teaching only love to our children is often difficult because most of us do not deeply believe that we are loving beings or that we ourselves are deserving of others' love. We project these feelings about ourselves outward, onto our children. And then we may experience our relationships with them as unloving.

As we reflect on our relationships with our parents and our children, and how these are so intertwined, one Attitudinal Healing concept in particular comes to mind: the idea that we create our realities from the thoughts and feelings we hold in our minds. Perhaps there is nowhere in life that this concept is more impactful than with our children.

We learn time and time again that the key to creating loving relationships is found through healing our relationships with ourselves. That is really the main ingredient of good parenting. So, then, how can we learn to love ourselves more consistently? We can begin by recognizing that we are not learning something new. Rather, all we need to do is *un-learn* the attitudes that are now blocking our awareness of our true essence, which is love.

Unlearning the old lessons, and thus healing the attitudes that block our awareness of love's presence in our lives, is not as difficult as it might seem. We start doing it by asking ourselves at moments when we are experiencing distress and pressure, Are my thoughts, feelings, words, and actions at this moment in harmony with one another? Or am I feeling one thing, thinking another thing, saying another, and doing still another? It is precisely this disharmony within ourselves that causes us pain, fear, and distress, and proliferates confusion in our children as they observe and learn from our actions.

When there is harmony among what we are feeling, thinking, saying, and doing, we experience no conflict within ourselves. Our relationships with ourselves and others, particularly our children, become open, loving, and tranquil. The love we express expands, extending out into the world.

The following positive questions help us heal the split mind. It can be helpful to remind ourselves of them whenever we are feeling disharmony within ourselves:

• *Do I recognize that my mind is split at this moment?* This statement makes us aware that our mind is holding on to two opposing views of one issue at the same time, exhibited in our erratic behavior.

• *Am I willing to change my thoughts?* We begin creating harmony and congruence in our minds when we stop finding value in continuing to support the attitudes that are causing us conflict. In doing so, it is helpful to remind ourselves that our thoughts and feelings are not created by people or events outside ourselves but that we create them ourselves.

• *Where am I not in harmony?* and *Am I thinking one thing and saying or doing another?* These questions allow us to pinpoint where and how our split mind is manifesting itself.

• *Am I willing to forgive?* Whenever we are experiencing the symptoms of a split mind, we can be certain that we are judging or condemning ourselves or someone else.

It is important to note here that we always have a choice about how we answer these questions and whether we want to choose peace of mind over conflict or love over fear. It is our own choice and no one else's. When we shift our attitudes toward a sincere desire to live our lives more honestly in all that we think, say, and do, we experience harmony and congruence within our minds and get relief from the pressure or distress we are feeling.

THE GUILTY PARENT

All too frequently we deflect the guilt we are experiencing within us onto our children. Piling guilt on our children and ourselves in this way robs us of the experience of love and is one of the ways we create disharmony within our own minds. When our children are not what we want them to be, or when in our own minds they fail to live up to our expectations, we feel that we are surely failures. Someone else, we may tell ourselves, could surely have done a better job of raising them. The guilt we experience at such times is a painful message. In our frustration we may turn right around and use that guilt to manipulate our kids into modifying their behavior, which only worsens the situation because we are then mixing together our own issues with theirs.

We often compare ourselves to models of families we see on television or read about in books or know only superficially in our daily lives. We forget that what we are seeing may only be a tiny fragment of the whole picture. Yet we grab hold of our guilt and tell us that if we were just a little bit more like these other people, maybe we wouldn't have to feel badly about ourselves. Comparing our own family to others' families in this way only confirms the depth of what we perceive as our own mishandling of the job.

There's another wonderful story told to us by Robert Young. He said that one day one of his daughters complained to him, "How come that you are so smart on television, solving really hard problems the family is having in just thirty minutes, but at home you are so slow?" Robert quickly replied, "Oh, on television I have good scriptwriters."

Our young people are constantly barraged with pressure to conform. They get it from us, their parents. They also get it from their own peers and the youth subculture in which they participate at some level every day. They are always faced with pressured choices that divert them from the paths that we would choose for them. But ultimately the choices are up to each of us.

OUR CHILDREN

Does teaching only love to our children mean coddling, spoiling, or overindulging them? Does it mean that we should speak to them only in a certain tone of voice, or that we should never correct them for fear that we might not appear loving? Does it mean that we should always try not to upset them, for fear that we would lose their, or someone else's, approval? The answer is no, because teaching love also means learning to say no. *"Teaching only love" should never be confused with permissiveness.*

The essence of teaching is offering, by word or by deed, a new or alternative piece of knowledge. If we wish to teach love, we do this by extending the love within us out into the world, with the realization that the essence of our being *is* love. We do this with the realization that when we communicate the content of our hearts and our minds to our children, we teach them that the essence of *their* being, too, is love.

GRANDPARENTING

Becoming a grandparent is like entering a whole new realm. In some ways it is like entering a hall of mirrors where everything is mirrored back at you from an entirely new perspective.

Recently, a close friend told me (Diane) that it wasn't until she had grandchildren that she finally understood what her own parents must have gone through when they had grandchildren. Along with the arrival of her two grandchildren she gained a deeper compassion and appreciation for our parents.

It is much harder to observe ourselves objectively while raising our own children than it is when we are spending time with our grandchildren. The generation between gives us perspective. We can see that parenting is never a perfect job. Each of us does the very best we know how at the time.

My mother, Phyllis Girard offers an interesting insight about the experience of being a grandparent. She says her guilt as a parent finally dissolved when she saw her grown children, and now her grandchildren and great grandchildren, and realized fully that she truly *did* do the very best that she could. With all the bleak realities of growing up, she also showed us the beauty. With all the opportunities to see scarcity, she showed us great abundance in the ways we might choose to see the world.

My mother lives the message she has bequeathed to her grandchildren and great-grandchildren—that your attitude about life and what it offers is one of your most precious possessions. When it is laced with gratitude for all the experiences you can learn from, then you are the wealthiest, most successful person in the world.

RESPONSE-ABILITY

When we think about the word *responsibility*, most of us make associations with concepts such as "duty" and "obligation." We would like to suggest a new way of thinking about this word, as *an ability to be responsive*, to be open and allow the natural flow of love, with no attempts to block it in any way.

If we want our children to grow up to be *responsible*, caring, and loving adults, we must first be *response-able* in our own thoughts and actions. We must care for our children in ways that reflect consistent harmony in what we think, say, and do. And above all, we must teach only love, for that is what we are and that is what they are too.

As parents, when we are confused about what to do, we can always choose to quiet our minds for a moment and be still. With the power of our love we can seek help and direction from within, from the guide that always rests in our heart. When we make the choice to be *response-able* to that inner voice, and learn to trust it, solutions to even the greatest challenges of parenting will come to us quite quickly and with clarity.

Affirmations

1. Let me always remember that children are teachers of love and patience.
2. Let me never rationalize that it is all right for me to hurt any child in any way.
3. Let me be reminded to love and let go of my children, every second of their lives.
4. Let me remember to demonstrate honesty in all my transactions, as a way of teaching honesty to my children.
5. I will love my children unconditionally and not base my love on their performance.
6. Since I know that guilt and love cannot coexist, I will resist all temptations to try to control my children through guilt.
7. I am willing to share my mistakes with my children, and I am willing to forgive them and myself for whatever mistakes we make.
8. I will not hold grievances against my children.
9. I will remember that my children are not my "possessions."
10. I will do everything I can to empower my children's growth, self-esteem, and independence.

❖

CHAPTER SIX

EDUCATION—WE TEACH WHAT WE WANT TO LEARN

*Remember always
that what you believe,
you will teach.*

EDUCATION—WE TEACH WHAT WE WANT TO LEARN

For most of us education is lifelong. Whether we are parents teaching our own children the most rudimentary skills of living, managers supervising employees in a new work procedure, professionals instructing patients or clients, a friend helping a friend study for a driving test, volunteers working in a classroom, or even when we are alone in our own studies, we find ourselves in roles as educators. Similarly, even as students in a classroom, at work, or anywhere else that learning is taking place, our own attitudes can contribute to creating an environment where both students and teachers can feel safe and inspired.

When you stop to think about it, we are always finding ourselves in learning situations, because the world itself is our classroom and each one of us is both a teacher and a student nearly every moment that we are awake. Thus the most inspiring principles of education are not just the business of teachers but of all of us. Taking a close-up look at the most powerful teaching experiences reveals specific ways we can all put the principles of Attitudinal Healing into practice whenever we are confronted with the opportunity to teach and learn.

BUILDING A NEW CURRICULUM

Although our society tends to measure a lot of things, such as performance skills in reading, writing, and arithmetic, perhaps one of the most important things we can teach our kids is how to communicate with each other, how to love one another, how to appreciate the differences between us, and how to raise the question for them, What is the purpose of life?

Perhaps the highest purpose in life is not to perform our skills but how to learn to listen, care for, help, and love others, and how to forgive others and ourselves. Perhaps the greatest skill we can learn in our educational process is how to live with each other peacefully, without fighting and without wars.

Dr. Janice E. Laine

Dr. Janice E. Laine has had over thirty years of experience as an educator. She has been very much on her own spiritual pathway during that time, and her experience in this can be a guiding light for us all. Among the many positions she has held is the directorship of the California State School for the Neurologically Handicapped.

I (Jerry) was a consultant for that school, and as soon as I stepped into the building, I felt an atmosphere of unconditional love and peace that was quite remarkable. I found that this was true for both students and staff. I felt a wonderful sense of harmony, and I immediately knew that this was a school dedicated to teaching love.

We recently had a chance to interview Janice, who is now consulting with high schools and middle schools on cultural change and school restructuring. She told us, "We do a lot of work helping teachers to develop new visions and to see themselves as members of a team. This means that they learn to see the value of letting go of the past when they have had a difficult encounter with another teacher or an administrator. I see that our job as consultants is to help educators create peaceful and loving environments, not only for their students but for themselves as well."

Janice went on to say, "We also try to help teachers identify conversations for *no possibilities*—that is, conversations that do not lead to a new future. These are communications that are *attacking* and defensive and that keep us stuck in the same vicious cycles. We support teachers in creating situations where everyone wins and we accomplish our visions. Of course I do my best to apply these same principles in my own life. I keep reminding myself that I can choose peace instead of conflict and love instead of fear. It is also helpful to remind ourselves that when kids are misbehaving, it is because of fear. It is important not to put them into negative categories. There is not a single day when forgiveness cannot play a very prime role in the schoolroom."

Palm Beach Community College

There seem to be many examples of teachers who bring their own spiritual beliefs into the classroom to create loving and caring environments where people are encouraged to learn and grow. There are also models for us to follow of people who are teaching spiritual values more directly.

One of the educational institutions where Attitudinal Healing has become quite popular is Palm Beach Community College, in Lake Worth, Florida. Attitudinal Healing is taught in an evening course by Kathleen McManus, whose students range in age from eighteen to seventy years. The class is learning to apply the principles of Attitudinal Healing in their personal and work lives. They are learning how to look at the world differently, how to change their perceptions, and how to take responsibility for their emotions and what they experience. Most of all the underlying emphasis is on the fact that forgiveness is the key to happiness. The class uses as its text the book *Love Is Letting Go of Fear* and also uses the audio-tapes from the same book.

LOVE AND COOPERATION

We can learn about the power of love and cooperation by having an educational system where teachers are themselves models for these very characteristics. It is possible that the heart of our educational system can become one in which children are learning how to live with each other cooperatively and harmoniously. Can all the performance skills we learn really be meaningful if we do not learn the way to live peacefully and cooperatively with each other?

It is possible to create environments where children can learn to believe in themselves, to believe that they are lovable not because of how they perform but because of what they are. There are already many bright lights in our schools, teachers who are demonstrating these concepts every day of their lives.

The concepts of Attitudinal Healing are proving to be very practical in the educational environment. That it is possible to transform fear into love is being demonstrated in many different schools. These schools are helping to emphasize the importance of removing the blocks to our feeling a sense of oneness with each other—regardless of the differences in our sex, race, economic status, or religious preference. They are helping to bring about a goal of joining rather than one of separation.

In classrooms where love and cooperation are emphasized, competition is being replaced by cooperation and collaboration. There is more and more room for communication that is focused on how we are alike rather than on how we are different. More attention is focused on a genuine appreciation for individual differences, with no need for negative or dehumanizing categorizations.

PRACTICAL APPLICATIONS

We have had the very gratifying experience of being able to consult with teachers, students, and administrators in a number of different school districts. As in any area of our lives where people with difficult challenges are trying to work very closely with one another, relationship problems arise. Along with those who have asked us to help them seek other ways of looking at the educational environment, we have learned much about the communication problems between teachers and teachers, teachers and principals, principals and superintendents, and between superintendents and boards of education. We have learned much as we worked with teachers and students on relationship difficulties at every level of their lives.

So many of the problems that arise seem to spring from the tendency to categorize people—one of the habits that any of us may find a great temptation when we are looking for ways to simplify the inner workings of complex institutions. When there are behavior problems, a child may quickly be labeled a "bad kid" or a "troublemaker." Where there is a parent who seems to be neglecting his or her child, there may be a temptation to label that parent "uncooperative" and perhaps even write the child off as a "lost cause." This not only causes much separation in our society, it makes it difficult for the person labeled to change, even when he or she wants to. As one student put it, "It's real hard to peel off those kinds of labels because they are in other people's minds, not your own. So after a while it gets so it feels like other people are doing everything they can to keep you from changing. You just want to give up."

It is possible to prevent labeling before it begins, as well as to remove labels that have already been put in place. In the school districts we have visited, one of the most helpful principles has been the idea that there really is another way of looking at the kinds of behavior that get negatively labeled. Rather than seeing kids as bad, teachers are learning to perceive them as fearful. This is based on the Attitudinal Healing concept that there are really only two emotions to consider in all our communications: We are being either loving or fearful, and the latter is really a call of help for love.

PEOPLE ARE EITHER LOVING OR FEARFUL, GIVING A CALL OF HELP FOR LOVE

Schools have found this concept to be extremely helpful. It is difficult to be compassionate when you are using negative labels with people. As a matter of fact, when we use negative labels, it is a form of attack.

We believe that it is possible to retrain our minds to believe that there are only two emotions: love and fear. This means that every thought we have in our minds comes either from love or from fear. What we see in the world is determined by our beliefs and our thoughts.

Rather than interpreting behavior and putting people into categories of whether they deserve our love or our anger, we can choose to resist the temptation to judge them based on our interpretations. We can choose to see everyone, adults and children, as either loving or giving a call of help for love.

Teachers are finding that when they recognize that a certain behavior of a child comes from fear, they can be compassionate and approach that child quite differently than before. And of course the same idea can be applied to communications with parents.

Our friend Hal Bennett, who has helped us in the editing of this book, relates the following story of an experience he had during his first job as a teaching assistant. That experience contains a valuable lesson in what we can do to respond to a child's fear, and perhaps help heal it, even when it has been expressed in destructive ways that we cannot condone.

The school was located in a very rough inner-city neighborhood, and many of the children were from an environment where there was often much more fear than love. There was one little girl named Trina who was particularly fearful. She was ten years old, and every day she came to school filled with anger. If other children even looked at her the wrong way, she was quite capable of starting a fight with them.

One day Trina gave a younger boy, Hal, a bloody nose. An older teacher, Mrs. Robbins, told Hal, "You take care of the bloody nose. I'll take care of Trina." As Hal watched, Mrs. Robbins took Trina's hands lovingly in hers and said, "Are you all right?"

Mrs. Robbins looked into Trina's face with love and caring, and what happened in the next moment seemed like a miracle. Trina's face suddenly softened, and then giant tears started running down her cheeks. A second later Trina threw her arms around Mrs. Robbins and hugged her tightly.

Over the next few weeks and months Trina's behavior began to change. Her fearful behavior was beginning to disappear. Where she had once been filled only with attack and defense, she was now becoming a peacemaker, helping other children to communicate in more loving ways.

Mrs. Robbins told Hal that she knew Trina's anger came from a pain deep in her heart. One of the most valuable lessons this teacher had learned from all her years of teaching was that love, not more anger and fear, helped the children heal and begin to see another way of looking at the world.

IN MY OWN DEFENSELESSNESS MY SAFETY LIES

Another concept that we frequently find helpful in schools, as elsewhere, is the value of learning to be defenseless. There are many situations where parents may come to school and, by all appearances, appear to be angry and attacking. When we perceive another person as attacking, our egos want to jump in and attack back; effective communication goes down the drain.

But we need not be limited to the ego's messages about how to respond to anger or attack. We can choose to change our perception and see that person, as in the story about Trina, as fearful and asking for help. Once again, we can choose to be compassionate, loving, understanding, and helpful.

When we choose to see another person as fearful rather than attacking, and we become defenseless, it opens our hearts up to reach out to that person and to find something that allows us to be joined with them. If we persist in seeing that person as only attacking us, we will defend ourselves and fight back. This perpetuates the cycle of separation.

COMMITMENT TO SERVE OTHERS

We find today that there are beginning to be more programs that are designed to create a sense of joining and self-esteem by helping others. These programs do much to impart what cooperation and collaboration are all about; they are devoid of competition because there is a joint goal and everyone plays an equal part.

Perhaps as time goes on, we will be able to see that love, cooperation, and collaboration are much more powerful teaching principles than fear and competition. It is here that we discover how we are alike rather than how we are different, and it is here that we begin to pay more attention to appreciating and accepting all of our varying levels of achievement as well as our individual differences.

At the Waldorf School in Santa Cruz, California, we have had the opportunity to visit educational programs that have fully incorporated community service into the educational curriculum for all grades. The lessons they have learned have much to offer all of us about the value of serving others.

At Waldorf teachers and students work together to provide nutritional lunches for the elderly. They work to help the homeless find food and shelter as well as medical care and work. They paint fences, walk pets, and do housework for older people or others who cannot do these things for themselves.

The goal of these programs is to bring about a sense of joining within the classroom and within the community. The goal is to be of service and to help each other and the community at large in creative ways. Feelings of self-worth and a raising of self-esteem are experienced by everyone the program touches.

There are no grades and there is no competition in this project. It is a project that is motivated from the heart, by love. Almost as an added value, students learn the most practical applications for the three R's—by calculating food quantities, ordering materials, writing letters to community members or institutions with whom they wish to cooperate, and organizing work groups.

We like to imagine what would happen throughout the world if schools began implementing programs like this one, committed to serving the community around them. Recently, Maryland implemented a statewide program for a volunteer community service as a basic requirement for graduation from both junior high and high school. What a wonderful way to potentially increase self-esteem and to experience oneself as contributing something good and significant to the world.

KIDS TEACHING KIDS

Over twenty years ago Dr. Keith Berry, I (Jerry), and others founded the Child Center, in Kentfield, California, which was devoted to helping children with learning disorders. I was particularly interested in being involved in this program because of my own learning difficulties in the past.

At the Child Center we found that most children with severe reading problems also suffered from poor self-images and low self-esteem, the result of their experiencing repeated failure in a highly competitive educational system. It occurred to us that if the children with learning problems could be given an opportunity to help others learn how to read, it would be helpful all around. We started a program in which third-graders helped first-graders with their studies. The first-graders enjoyed learning reading skills from children who were older but had many of the same difficulties they themselves had. And the third-graders were able to experience themselves as not being "dumb" or "unskilled" at all but as having knowledge and a sense of caring that allowed them to make a positive contribution in other children's lives.

At the Child Center we constantly emphasized positive reinforcement, such as always looking for examples in which a child was succeeding or doing well, rather than focusing on the negative feedback of pointing out only where children were failing. It was particularly gratifying to us to see that as the children's self-esteem rose, they also began to be more and more successful in their learning. They also showed more and more appreciation for their own and other people's differences.

All the children at the Child Center were learning, at an early age, that as we learn to help others, we also learn to help ourselves, which is the Attitudinal Healing principle that says that giving and receiving are truly the same.

KIDS HELPING KIDS AROUND GRIEF

For years we have sent staff members from the Center for Attitudinal Healing to schools where a student or teacher had died. Many times the death of a person whom everyone in a school has known can bring up emotions that most of us find extremely difficult to work through. Yet doing so can be extremely important for young people who have lost a schoolmate or close friend for the first time and may have little or no experience in what it is to grieve. One day it occurred to us that a child from our center who had experienced the death of a brother or sister could be even more helpful to students than adult staff members.

This program proved to be very successful. The children from our center spoke the language of the other kids in the schools, and they spoke with authority on the subject, since they had recently gone through the process of grieving for a relative or loved one who had recently died.

Today at the Center this is a continuing program. Our children have become important teachers, serving students in a great many schools where the experience continues to enforce their own healing process. They become teachers for others, not only in helping with the emotions children experience around the subject of death but around other issues as well. For example, in one classroom there was a young student who was going to have his leg amputated because of cancer. There was a second child from our center who had already undergone the same operation. He went to the first child's class and met with the children. We cannot even begin to describe how helpful he was to the students and the teacher, answering every question that a person could possibly have about the operation and the recovery that followed.

TEACHING FEAR

As the end of this century approaches, it sometimes seems that old systems and institutions are breaking down so quickly that it is difficult to keep up with them. Ways of life that we may have considered secure and enduring are suddenly gone. We continue to experience major shifts in our daily lives, ranging from "mild aggravations" to "sheer and utter chaos."

An educational system often reflects the society that it serves. In our society today we see a wildly increased incidence of drug abuse, rape, incest, emotional, physical, and sexual abuse of both children and adults, murder, wars, and conflicts with different factions within the society. We cannot help but ask, What is the world teaching our children? All the evidence seems to be saying that the world is teaching fear instead of love.

Our motion picture and television programs are frequently filled with violence and destruction. More politicians and business people than ever before seem to be landing in jail for their illegal activities. We are spending billions of dollars more on the instruments of war than we are on education or humanistic endeavors. Is it any wonder that all of us are confused about our goals and what we should value in our lives?

When you stop to think about it, is it any wonder that so many parents, teachers, school administrators, and students are feeling defensive, angry, and are suffering from low self-esteem? We are living in an environment that is filled with fear. This fear infiltrates every avenue of life and shows up in very powerful ways in our educational environments.

In spite of the many challenges, some of which seem quite overwhelming at times, education continues to attract courageous and dedicated young women and men, who are convinced that they can make a contribution. They care, and they feel that their beliefs and determination can take them and their students on the long journey to the other side of fear.

CHANGES

Whenever we are faced with major changes in our lives, many strong emotions come up. For some of us these emotions include a lot of fear, the concern that we will no longer be in control in areas of our lives that had once seemed familiar and secure. That experience is often followed by depression. For others, however, the changes bring much excitement, creativity, and optimism as they contemplate the uncharted waters ahead.

Education itself has undergone many changes. There have been shifts in the methods for teaching different subjects. There have been shifts in staffing patterns, teachers' benefits, the numbers of students per classroom, and increased record keeping that adds to teachers' already large burden of responsibilities.

Teachers, parents, and administrators have in many cases worked together to meet the challenges of our society head on and to orchestrate the changes that become necessary in the schools. Yet confusion and burnout continue to plague teachers and cast a dark shadow over the original intentions that brought them to this profession.

BURNOUT

We find that the field of education is a microcosm of life's macrocosm, providing us with opportunities to explore new and creative ways of communicating. So often we are taught to think of education as a one-way street: The teacher gives out the information and the student takes it in. Yet the principles of Attitudinal Healing teach us that all output and no input leads to an early burnout, not only for the teacher but for the student as well.

We have found that in classrooms where teachers and students are equally excited about being together day in and day out, there is the belief that learning is a two-way street. There is a sense of joining, and the classroom becomes an exciting and creative environment for all. When teachers come into a classroom with the belief that students are major contributors in the learning experience, young people feel validated and are encouraged to grow, not just in their own right but in terms of helping others to grow too. Cooperation and oneness replace competition and separation.

When teachers go into a classroom with the belief that they are the only ones with something of value to impart, students tend to become passive, noncontributors. This leads to high stress for the teacher, low learning performance on the part of students, and an early burnout.

In classrooms where the teacher believes they are the only contributors, a vicious cycle occurs. The teacher starts out with set goals in mind, that they will consider themselves "successful" only if the students are able to accurately feed back exactly the information being taught. When the student fails to do this, the teacher may feel compelled to try even harder.

It seems that the harder we try to control what is being learned in the classroom, the deeper the feelings of separation, isolation, ingratitude, and helplessness grow. As the latter occurs, learning drops off to a mere trickle, and discipline problems grow greater and greater. It is difficult to turn this pattern around, because the teacher still believes that the solution is to be found in getting the students to "feed back" exactly what the books or the instructors say they should learn.

In this kind of unsuccessful classroom teachers often begin to feel very angry, though their egos may keep this hidden from their conscious minds. Their egos begin telling them that the reason they are not successful is that the students are refusing to cooperate. The students become the teachers' adversaries, or even downright "enemies," because they appear to be the cause of the teachers not achieving their goals.

So what is the solution when this happens? Does it mean that the teacher should not try so hard? Does it mean that the teacher should give up her or his academic goals for the students? Should the teacher lower standards? No. In fact, quite the contrary is true. The best way to explain this is by providing an example. The following story about Alison and Marilyn may be helpful.

Alison and Marilyn

Alison and Marilyn began teaching in the same school at about the same time, about ten years before we heard of them. Their stories have much to teach us all about how attitudes can contribute either to burnout or to a continuing love and excitement about one's profession. They are equally dedicated, talented, and experienced. When they started, they were equally enthusiastic about their profession. However, a decade later Alison is still excited about teaching and is actively exploring new curricula and new ways of learning. By contrast, Marilyn has just resigned, feeling depressed, resentful, and painfully burnt out.

What is it, then, that makes the difference? Here are two people who began on parallel tracks yet their eventual destinations turned out to be very, very different. Certainly the daily overloads of school politics and administrative red tape take their toll. But both of them had these things to contend with. How did Alison not only survive it all but continue to have a rewarding, positive experience while her associate has burned out and quit?

It wasn't what was going on in the external world that made the difference for these two young teachers; it was what was going on inside them. Their *attitudes* and their goals differed greatly, and that is what made the difference.

Marilyn, who finally burned out, had a very specific picture in her mind of what must happen in the classroom for her to feel that she was successful. Her idea was that the students should respect her and like her, just as she had respected and liked her teachers when she was a student. She wanted them to take in all the information she imparted to them and to feed it back to her on essays and tests exactly as she had in mind. She had a similar plan for the administration and her co-workers. When any of these ideals weren't met, by students or others, Marilyn consciously and subconsciously started looking for somebody or something to blame: the students, the administrators, other teachers, parents, society, or herself.

Alison, however, had a very different set of goals in her work. This goal was always attainable because it was always within the realm of her control. She chose to make her own peace of mind her only goal. All other efforts were expressions of her *intentions,* which sometimes worked out and sometimes didn't. She seemed to have boundless energy to just be *present* with her students and to feel joined with them, as opposed to playing an adversarial role. Because she was not attached to the immediate results, she rarely drained her own energy.

Alison had learned an important Attitudinal Healing principle. She learned that we can choose not to base our happiness on how someone else performs. This should not be confused with not caring. On the contrary, she chose *not* to give her power away to her students, co-workers, parents, or the administration of the school where she taught. Because she didn't set herself or her students up to be each other's "enemies," she was able to motivate, guide, and educate them while accepting the choices they made for themselves. In accepting the students' individual choices, Alison was actually "teaching what she wanted to learn"— which in this case was unconditional love, the ability to support and love others without setting out conditions that they must meet. She certainly set up guidelines for them, but she did not threaten to withdraw her love or attention from them when they didn't meet them.

Alison found that she could learn about and practice unconditional love in the classroom in a way that would be beneficial to everyone. To have unconditional love for her students did not mean that she supported their insanity. It meant that she let go of her judgments and criticisms of others. When this was done, she went inside, seeking counsel from within, and asked what it was that she should think, say, and do in each new situation. More often than not, clear, definitive guidelines emerged. They were fresh and creative answers that came from a place of unconditional love, not cluttered with any negative feelings of anger, disappointment, or predetermined scripts that she had written for other people.

ONE GOAL

As we shift focus in our lives, choosing peace of mind as our only goal, we are able to let go of the unattainable goals we might have for changing other people or "the world out there." The lesson we learn in teaching, as in all relationships in our lives, is that the most we can ever do with our desire to change others is to manipulate them into complying with our wishes for a while. True change ultimately comes out of inspiration and love, not out of pressure and fear.

It is very easy for teachers to become discouraged when they feel that they have been very loving and caring with a student yet major behavior difficulties continue. It is important to remember that the central core of love is patience. We have heard a number of teachers tell us that years later their most difficult student came to visit them to say that they were the teacher who made the difference. Certainly the student's behavior at school at the time would never have suggested that.

As we learn to love, to give our talents and ourselves without the attachments of our judgments and negative thoughts, we find ourselves with unbounded inspiration and energy, fully empowered to create and act in the world. We find ourselves giving and receiving in ways that are exciting for everyone concerned—student, teacher, and on out into the circle of parents, other teachers, administrators, and the community at large. As we learn to share ourselves with others, we begin to experience the role of teacher and student constantly shifting and interchanging, because we are teaching what we want to learn.

Affirmations
1. I choose to remember that I teach what I want to learn.
2. People I meet each day are either loving or fearful, giving a call of help for love.
3. We are all equally teachers and students to each other.
4. What I see, teach, and learn in the world is determined by my beliefs and thoughts.
5. I can choose to teach love or to teach fear.

CHAPTER SEVEN

❖

BODY ATTITUDES

*The body is endangered
by the mind
that hurts itself.*

THE BODY

Today more and more people are enjoying the many benefits of having a sense of harmony between mind, body, and spirit. The realization that our attitudes toward ourselves have something to do with how we treat our bodies has become widely accepted. We are seeing that our thoughts and beliefs about who and what we are affect our bodies in no uncertain terms.

BODY VERSUS SPIRIT

We don't often ask the question, What is the body? And yet much of our thinking and behavior are dependent on how we answer that question. There are some people who would answer that the body is only a glob of protoplasm, a form that continues to change and then eventually disappears. Others might say that the body is but a temporary home for our spiritual being, which continues to be present forever.

The big question is How do we wish to interpret the body? Do we choose to interpret it and the world only through its eyes or through the eyes of the spirit? We see the illusion of separation when we are holding on to the belief that the body is all there is and that when it dies, that's the end of the line.

When we believe that we are spiritual beings, we can then see the body as a temporary vehicle for bringing about joining, through the extension of love. When we use spiritual vision as a way of seeing, we can know that there is an everlasting joining of body, mind, spirit, and love.

When we go to a museum to look at paintings, some people might concentrate more on the frame than on the painting. Likewise, in life, many of us concentrate on the frame—the body—rather than on the picture, the love and spirit that are within the body but not limited to it. How we live our lives may depend on whether we focus on the *frame* or on the picture within the frame.

How We Relate to Our Bodies

The relationships we have with our bodies are direct reflections of how we answer questions such as What is the purpose of my body? How do I see my body and for what is it to be used? Who's in charge here? Am I my body and is my body me? Or am I much more than just my body? Does my mind control my body, or vice versa?

Often we may mistakenly believe that our minds are in our bodies and that our bodies control us. We are frequently in a state of confusion, thinking, My body is doing this, or That person's body is doing that. We therefore see the body as a vehicle for attack and separation rather than as a vehicle for love and joining. Likewise whenever we equate ourselves or others with the body, we ultimately wind up feeling depressed because we find it so difficult to control other people and their bodies.

The Body as a Positive or Negative Idol

Our minds are often in conflict, believing that our inner peace is always determined by the state of our bodies. We are in a state of confusion, believing that our bodies are actually capable of making decisions and telling us how we feel. We do not want to believe that, in actuality, our minds control our bodies and give all conscious and unconscious commands.

We can think of our bodies either as negative idols—something we hate—or as positive idols—something on which we fixate and worship. Either way we use our bodies to make us feel isolated, abandoned, and vulnerable to attack by other bodies.

As we let go of the false sense of identity we associate with the physical form, our body becomes our friend. I (Diane) vividly recall a recent trip we made to Hawaii after a long time away from the sun.

I was walking down the beach one afternoon on the coast of Maui and began to notice other sunbathers around me. If you want to experience confusion about your reality, just visit a Hawaiian beach where people have developed their bodies to the point of an art form. As I walked along the sand that day, I absentmindedly began compiling a long list of all the incredible body assets possessed by the other women I saw. I noted everything from small hips and thighs to flat stomachs, toned buttocks, and smooth, beautifully bronzed skin. At the same time I began compiling a second list of all my own defects and how I just didn't measure up.

What had started out as a pleasant, peaceful walk turned into a volcano of depression as I dove for my large beach towel to cover up my imperfections. My self-image was decimated as my mind focused only on my body, limiting my identity to my overweight, undertoned, aging body.

While I felt quite upset with myself, I also became quite fascinated by the tricks my split mind was able to play. Even as I was attacking my body with my laundry list of its obvious shortcomings, I was also making every person with a beautiful body my enemy, reducing them to being *only* bodies.

What a lesson I received that day! Recognizing my insanity, I made a very conscious choice to begin "recovering" myself with love. I took another walk down the beach, and with each step I took, I focused my mind on a different area of my body, surrounding it with light as I restored it to a place of love in my heart and in my mind.

As I walked along the beach that day, I also surrounded everyone I saw with love, reminding myself that we are not just our bodies and that comparisons are malignant, sickening our souls. As I walked along the warm sand that time, I began feeling more and more peaceful, more and more at one with everyone and everything around me. It was one of the most liberating, effective, and lasting exercises I have ever experienced.

OUR GUILTY THOUGHTS CAN ATTACK OUR BODIES

When we neglect our bodies, when we fail to nurture them with daily exercise, healthy foods, rest, and relaxation, it is usually because we have negative thoughts about ourselves. These negative thoughts usually involve guilt and blame. There are times when because of our guilt we actually end up imprisoning ourselves in our bodies. Holding on to guilt can cause us to feel that we need to punish ourselves. Usually we do this without thinking, attacking ourselves as if our bodies had become our enemies, resulting in pain and illness.

We all carry mental images of ourselves in our minds. Sometimes these are positive images, but many times they may be negative ones. When these mental pictures are negative, framed with unforgiving thoughts, both mind and body can suffer. One of the effects that we frequently see when these negative images are maintained over a long period of time is backache.

Back Problems

For many years before the two of us met, we each carried heavy loads of guilt and depression, resulting in back problems that at times forced us to be completely inactive for several days in a row. What we learned about ourselves was that every time we experience back pain, it is because, consciously or unconsciously, we are making negative judgments about ourselves or other people. Our backs and necks are our "weak links," signaling us to pay more attention to what we are thinking and feeling.

Since we have learned this, we have begun to pay attention to our pain very early on. At the first twinge of any pain we stop our activities, sit down in a quiet place, and become still. Then we begin to explore any attack thoughts we may be having, either against ourselves or against other people. We find that we are usually successful in identifying and then experiencing the anger we are having with the person or situation. We then go to work on having a willingness to forgive the other person and ourselves. It doesn't work every time, but we are really impressed by how rapidly, and frequently, the pain dissolves along with the inner turmoil we may have been experiencing.

Pain in the Neck

Pain in the neck is not only a common ailment, it is also a very common expression of tension, friction, and suppressed anger. Perhaps one of the reasons it is so common is that many of us carry negative and judgmental thoughts about other people in our minds as we go through the day. We may feel guilty about these hostile, unforgiving thoughts, even if our guilt is only at a subconscious level.

The self-punishment that comes from this guilt can end up as a pain in the neck. In our unconscious mental state, however, it seems as though it is the *other person* who is the real "pain in the neck."

We believe that the pain is the result of things that happen outside ourselves, and as long as we choose to believe this vision of our lives, we remain in the position of being victims, unable to do anything to change our lives. The angry, blaming, unforgiving thoughts we hold in our minds and in our bodies ultimately cause pain only to ourselves.

Some years ago we were teaching a workshop in Australia. A working mother raised her hand and asked for some help with the intense pain in the back of her neck that she had been experiencing for about three weeks. The lesson her experience taught us all turned out to be one in which everyone with chronic pain can perhaps discover the source of great comfort.

Even from across the room we could easily see that she was tense and uncomfortable. We asked her if she would be willing to explore what had been going on in her life when she first experienced this pain. At first she could not remember. Then all of a sudden she said, "Oh, yes, now I remember!" She went on to tell us the following story:

"My teenage daughter was giving me a bad time. She had stayed out too late, and I grounded her. She was really being loud, ugly, and difficult. I was exasperated with her and told her that when she was in this state of mind, she was really a pain in the neck."

Without skipping a beat, she went on, sharing a long list of other difficulties she was having in her relationship with her daughter. We waited a moment, then politely asked her, "Did you hear yourself say that your daughter could sometimes be a pain in the neck?"

She quickly replied, "No, I didn't hear myself say that." She paused for just a second, then added, "Oh, my God, that's exactly what I said!"

As the young mother shared her story with the group, other people in the workshop spoke out, offering their support and love. One person assured her of how normal it was to have feelings of frustration around one's teenagers. Another person shared that it was no sin to occasionally feel that your own children are a pain in the neck—or even further down the spine than that. Even as we watched, the tension seemed to dissolve from the woman's face.

At the end of the day this young working mother came up to us smiling. The pain in her neck had disappeared as she let go of the deep guilty feelings she had been burdening herself with for being angry with her daughter. Surprisingly, the anger she felt dissolved along with her guilt, and she was suddenly open to exploring other ways of looking at the situation.

THE BODY AND THE MEDIA

Many of us have allowed ourselves to be highly influenced by the media, making what they consider to be "acceptable" or "beautiful" our standards for judging ourselves and others. As we buy into *their* standards of judgment, we literally give *our* power away, measuring the whole world by what we see, hear, or read in newspapers, magazines, radio, and television. The result is that we end up feeling unhappy about ourselves and many other people in our lives. Measured against the media standards, we are too fat, too thin, too short, or too tall. There are parts of our bodies that we don't like, and as we dwell on what we don't like, those parts become our enemies. There are so many of us who end up hating the size or shape of our noses, teeth, lips, ears, eyes, breasts, genitals, buttocks, thighs, and so on.

When we adopt the standards for bodies created in the media, we fall into the trap of never being completely satisfied with how our bodies look. We end up always striving to be like someone else or even like a superhuman ideal that we have created in our minds from a whole collection of media standards. As we create these idols in our minds, we are literally setting ourselves up to feel separate and fearful, seeing both our bodies and the external world as our enemies.

Wanting Our Bodies to Be Different

When I (Jerry) was an adolescent, I was the proverbial skinny guy on the beach who wanted to look like Mr. America, the current version of which was Charles Atlas. At another time in my life, I am still embarrassed to say, I wanted to look like John Wayne. I was convinced that my muscles were too small, my nose too big, and . . . my toes were ugly. I really didn't like my body at all, and these perceptions mirrored what I thought of my personality. I grew up thinking of myself as an ugly duckling, inside and out. I believed that the only way I could ever love my body was if it suddenly changed to be like John Wayne's or Charles Atlas's. The lesson my story offers is that it is not our bodies but our attitudes that need to change, if we wish to experience love.

Unfortunately my perceptions about the way I looked didn't evaporate as I moved through adolescence into adulthood. As a matter of fact I went through many years being

an active alcoholic, during which time I tried to destroy my
body and nearly succeeded in killing myself. Negative self-
images go deep and affect us greatly until we heal our relationships with ourselves.

To be perfectly honest with myself and you, I would have
to admit that it has only been since 1975, while I have been
on a spiritual path, that I have begun to accept my body
and let it be my friend rather than my enemy. And what a
difference this new way of looking at the world has made
in my life. I realize that I am not by any means alone in my
story and that many of you reading this book can fully identify with what I am saying.

Gregg Johnson

We wanted to explore some health practitioners' views of
how to create healthy relationships with our bodies. We
talked with Gregg Johnson, a gifted physical therapist who
has a practice in Kentfield, California. We interviewed him
at the Marin Back and Spine Clinic, where Gregg and his
talented and loving staff continually demonstrate principles
very much like those we find in Attitudinal Healing, only
applied to the physical body.

Gregg has noticed that as people become more aware of
the relationship between physical fitness and overall health,
they have taken more and more responsibility for their own
well-being. They have begun paying more attention to diet
and have eliminated nicotine, alcohol, and drug con-
sumption.

When people come to Gregg for relief from pain, or to
increase limited movements in their bodies, they are often
able to reflect on how these are linked with their emotions
and perceptions about themselves. Gregg strongly believes
that one of the most important aspects of the healing process
he offers is to help patients believe in themselves and to
believe that nothing is impossible.

Gregg has a strong belief in the existence of a Higher
Power, and he feels it is not possible to separate the physical
from the spiritual aspects of healing. Although he certainly

does not try to influence his patients where their spiritual beliefs are concerned, he does pray for guidance that he can serve God's will in his work with his clients.

He told us that he does his best to see the essence of love in everyone he sees. Through honesty and integrity, and by establishing a caring, loving relationship, he demonstrates harmony in his own life that radiates outward.

In his own life, Gregg is careful to nurture and care for his body in every way he can. In addition to watching his diet and stress levels, he rides his bike to and from work, a distance of twelve miles. What motivates him is his belief that the body is a temple of the spirit.

The first principle of Attitudinal Healing is "The essence of our being is love." What this means is that our true identity is a spiritual one and that what we are is love. It is a belief that we are not limited to the physical body, and that our true identity, being love, is formless and timeless.

When we accept our true identity as a spiritual one, we can then recognize that we are all interconnected, that we are all expressions of the Universal Mind, to which we are all joined. It is a reality where there is no separation, only joining.

Within this belief system the physical body is seen as a vehicle for helping, caring, and being of service to each other. While interviewing Gregg Johnson it became clear to us that he is very much in touch with his own spiritual identity. Perhaps he has such a successful practice because he does his best to bring about a balance of body, mind, and spirit, not only in his own life but in the lives of all those around him.

WHEN FATIGUE IS A STATE OF MIND

Most of us know what it means to feel overworked, exhausted, and irritable at the end of the day, like a worn-out heap of protoplasm. Some of us have also experienced how it is to feel so tense and exhausted that we can hardly wait to get home and climb into bed. We are absolutely convinced that we have only enough energy to crawl between the covers and collapse.

And then, as we come into the house, the phone rings. We answer it to be greeted by a very dear friend who's in town just for the night. All of a sudden we forget the long, tiring day we've just struggled through and are suddenly full of pep, excited about going out on the town with our friend.

What happened? What was it that occurred to make that shift from utter exhaustion to happy anticipation of spending time with our friend? In those few moments our bodies did not change. What changed was our attitude. We developed a new focus, shifting our attention completely away from our body and the activities of the day. Rather than being preoccupied with the past hours of demanding and exhausting work, filled with frustration and negativity, we are now focused on sharing time with a friend, which will be fun.

As we take a shower and get dressed, we find that we have gotten a second wind. All our fatigue has disappeared, almost as if by magic. That second wind actually blew through as a shift in attitude, refreshing our mind before it finally filtered down to our body, refreshing that as well.

The power of the mind is unlimited. That power is manifest in the realization that as we change our minds, we change our lives. That power is always within our grasp as we learn to discipline our minds by making very conscious choices about what we think, say, and do.

Alternative Approaches

In our workaholic pasts we weren't always very good, seeming to put ourselves last on the list. We have both found, over the years, that when we do not take care of ourselves, our mental, physical, and spiritual energy all seem to diminish.

It used to be that we would wake up every morning with a list of things to do that was impossible to accomplish that day. Each day we would jump out of bed and jump onto a treadmill of endless activities and commitments, exhausting ourselves as we tried to complete the long list of things we believed we had to do. We would become so involved with the busy-ness of the day that there didn't seem to be a moment to take a walk or do any kind of regular physical exercise.

In response to our request for advice about ways we might take responsibility for nourishing ourselves, a dear friend once told us a story that helped us get on the right track.

He said to think about that razor you shave with each day. You continue to shave day after day, and all is going along very well. After some time, however, the razor begins to get dull. And it gets duller and duller. No longer doing the job well, it actually begins tearing at the skin until it becomes worse than useless in performing the job for which it was intended. If one is to keep the razor doing its job well and not causing damage, one must take the time to maintain the razor and keep it sharp.

He said to think of ourselves as that razor. We go along just great for a time, but then we start getting duller and duller from fatigue and lack of nourishment. We forget about the daily maintenance that keeps us in good shape, and we become less effective and increasingly unhappy. Stopping and taking time for ourselves is not only a good idea, it is absolutely mandatory if we hope to continue our work in the world.

Whenever we are tempted to create overly busy schedules for ourselves, we think about his advice. We no longer feel guilty about taking time off to care for ourselves and each other because we now know that we are doing it not only for ourselves but for everyone else we will encounter in our lives.

A WAY THAT WORKS FOR US

We thought it might be helpful to share with you some of the things that we have personally found to be helpful in bringing about a balance of body, mind, and spirit. We are not necessarily recommending this for you, but perhaps you will find that you will want to integrate some of the things we do into your own plan. We awaken at 5:00 A.M. during the week since we find the early-morning hours a very gentle and peaceful time, perfect for greeting the new day and getting in touch with our spirits.

When we stop and think about our own lives, there is no question in our minds that the most important thing of all is our relationship with the Power that created us. That relationship comes before anything or anyone else and is a very integral part of the relationship we (Diane and Jerry) share with each other as a couple. Prior to getting out of bed we say a short prayer from *A Course in Miracles* that reminds us of who and what we are and helps us set our single goal for the day. The prayer goes like this:

I am not a body; I am free
For I am still as God created me.
I want the peace of God
The peace of God is everything that I want
The aim of all my living here.
The end that I seek
My purpose, my function, and my life
While I abide where I am not at home.[1]

Experiencing this prayer each morning is like setting the rudder of our boat so that we can be crystal clear about our course and our goal for the day. With peace of mind as our only goal we experience no conflicting goals that would bring confusion into our lives. When peace of mind is our only goal, we begin to see the things we wish to accomplish in a different perspective. We recognize our wishes as *intentions*; we focus on them, and they receive our attention, but we are not attached to the final results.

Following our brief prayer, we do some stretching exer-

cises and meet again at 6:00 A.M. We read a passage from
A Course in Miracles and then meditate for twenty minutes.
Afterward we take a very brisk forty-minute silent medita-
tion walk.

We are very fortunate because we live in an area where
we are surrounded by wonderful trees, flora, and wildlife.
So when we are at home, our mornings are particularly
nourishing. However, much of the time we are on the road,
and our travels take us to hotels in large cities. Even in the
city we find that our early-morning walks nurture us and
help us to keep connected with our spiritual identity.

We have a light breakfast, consisting mostly of fruit. Then
we turn off our telephones and write from 8:00 A.M. until
1:00 P.M. When we are at home, we spend time at the Center
and also talking with or having meetings with people who
are in crisis or for a myriad of other reasons.

In the late afternoon we take a short walk, go for a bicycle
ride, or play tennis. In the evening we again take some time
to quiet our minds and meditate.

We are finding that by taking time to nurture ourselves
in this way, we feel much more energy, patience, and love
for all our relationships. We have finally included ourselves
among the people toward whom we wish to be kind and
loving.

When traveling, we try to eat only healthy foods, primarily
salads, soups, fruits, and nuts. We concentrate on creating
time in our often long, busy, and demanding days to quiet
our minds to receive spiritual renewal and to treat our bodies
with gentle physical exercise.

Once we experienced the value of changing our priorities
in the ways we have described, we found it was not at all
difficult to maintain our new schedule. We started by actually writing down our activities in our appointment books,
for example, writing in "Take a walk" for the 5:00 P.M. time
slot each day. Once it was put down in black and white, we
found ourselves fully honoring our taking care of ourselves
as a priority for that time, and we did our utmost to let
nothing else interfere.

We find that our new routine brings a lot of joy into

our lives. *The discipline has actually increased our freedom.* It reminds us not to take ourselves quite so seriously as we walk a bit more lightly on the journey that our present lives represent.

BODY, MIND, AND SPIRIT

Today there seems to be much more evidence that people want to concentrate not just on their bodies but on finding a sense of balance in their lives. Having left behind the days of "Me first," "I want it all," and "Let it all hang out," people everywhere are finding that to be really effective in the world, it is necessary for them to nourish some aspect of the body, the mind, and the spirit each and every day.

When we begin accepting our true identity as spiritual, what follows is that we are no longer limited to our physical being. The body becomes a vehicle for the expression of our spiritual essence. We cease making our bodies idols, though we respect, love, and honor them in ways that help us maintain harmony with all the aspects of our being.

Affirmations

1. I will look at my body as my friend and not as my enemy.
2. I will remember that my mind controls my body and not vice versa.
3. I choose not to attack my body by having any condemning thoughts about myself or others.
4. I will remember that the essence of my being is spirit and that my life is not limited to the reality of my body.
5. Today I will concentrate on the love I give to others rather than on my perceptions about our bodies.
6. Today I will make every effort to love my own body just as it is.
7. Today I will be more open to ways that I might bring more harmony between my mind, spirit, and body.

❖

CHAPTER EIGHT

ATTITUDES TOWARD SPORTS

*No longer conscious of my movement, I discovered
a new unity with nature. I had found a new source
of power and beauty, a source I never dreamed existed.*

—ROGER BANNISTER
(first person to break the four-minute mile)

Competence Versus Competition

Today our attitudes toward sports are certainly wide and varied. But more and more athletes are being motivated by a desire to be the best they can be rather than simply better than anyone else. They see athletics as a way to develop body, mind, and spirit, believing in a limitless world and experiencing the essence of their being joined with the whole. Surely this is expressed in the words of Roger Bannister, quoted at the beginning of this chapter, where he reflects on the sense of unity being connected with a source of power and beauty that he had never dreamed might exist.

Even out-and-out competition is beginning to be seen in a new light, not as a way of proving yourself to be better or worse than another but as a personal challenge that presses athletes to reach deep inside and find the very best in themselves that they can. This new athlete views the competitor not as an adversary or an enemy to be defeated at all costs but as a partner sharing a goal, a catalyst that prompts both of them to do their very best.

Benefits of a Positive Attitude

More and more we see the sports world evolving, being used as a form of social interaction, a way for communities to come together, to remind us all of how much we share as human beings, even when we are rooting for different teams. Often, too, our participation in sports activities, whether as players or as spectators, can provide a healthy release of tensions that have been stored in our bodies as a result of the pressures of day-to-day living.

Sports take many forms in our society today. For some it

means walking by themselves or with a friend or loved one. For others it means jogging, running, hiking, bicycling, mountain climbing, rowing, bowling, or swimming. The goals so many people are finding is that any sports activity can teach us about ourselves, often revealing to us how doing the very best you can is its own reward.

So many benefits can come out of even a modest program of walking. Depression and anxiety are lifted away. Emotional and psychological energies increase, and we become more optimistic about life. On a deep intuitive level we find ourselves developing a new appreciation for our bodies as vehicles for the spirit.

LETTING GO OF THE PAST

Changing your mind about failure, learning from the difficult experiences of your life, and then letting go of them all become imperative if we want to participate in sports and enjoy the experience. And the lessons we learn in our athletic activities carry over into every aspect of our lives. Regardless of the sport, be it golf, tennis, or anything else, being attached to our past failures only fosters more failure. It is certainly important to learn from our past performances how we can do better and not repeat the same mistakes over again. However, unless we focus on what we do right, even though it may appear to be overshadowed by what we did wrong, we are doomed to repeat our failures. Sports teach us the fine art of not being afraid to look at what went wrong and to correct our course without judging ourselves as bad, stupid, clumsy, or uncoordinated. We begin to see that it really is our own mind and our own scoreboard, and we can choose to let go of our ego's script for us.

SPECTATOR SPORTS

There is something almost magical about the way spectator sports can take us out of ourselves for a time and separate us from our worries and cares. It can also be wonderful and healthy to let it all hang out, yelling and screaming, cheering for our team, expressing our anger, joy, disappointment, and sense of victory along with a group that shares these strong emotions with us. It can serve as a healthy outlet for pent-up emotions.

For many people, watching an athletic activity provides them with the opportunity to express emotions in a safe way, a way that will not harm others. My (Jerry's) father was a wonderful teacher in this regard. When I was growing up, he had one night a week in which he was free to go his own way. Every Thursday night he went to the wrestling matches, and sometimes he would take me with him. Although I enjoyed being with my dad, I really hated the brutality of the matches.

My dad, on the other hand, loved the fights. Whenever I suggested to him that they were fake, he would tell me I was crazy and defend their authenticity. As I became an adult, I also began to realize that my father, a meek and mild-tempered man, had no real outlets for the frustration he felt running his own business and having a family that was not always peaceful or easy to deal with.

I am sure that the Thursday-night wrestling matches allowed my dad to express pent-up emotions that he believed he couldn't express in other ways. Knowing that he could express himself Thursday nights, he was better able to control feelings of anger he experienced at home and in his business.

TEAM SPORTS

We live in the San Francisco Bay Area. Everyone who lives in this area knows that the last game of the regular football season, the big game between the University of California and Stanford, is one that either team can win, regardless of their wins and losses up to that point. The major factor that determines the outcome, of course, is attitude.

The team that experiences itself as a single unit, with no

separation between its members, the one that is most successful in using active imagination and mental imagery to
picture itself playing well together and winning, is often the
one that ends up the victor. This demonstrates that winning
is an attitude based on learning from the past and living in
the present.

An essential ingredient for a winning attitude is the ability
to learn from experience and then let go of the past. Success
is a current state of mind. Those who have watched the San
Francisco Forty Niners have seen the miraculous relationship that Montana and Rice have. We believe that their success is not just due to long hours of practice and hard work.
Their minds are so joined that each one knows where the
other person will be and what he will do, in a way that their
physical senses and brains could never do alone.

Several years ago Michael Murphy wrote a book called
The Psychic Side of Sports. In that book he collected hundreds
of quotes from some of the world's greatest athletes, who
described what they considered to be spiritual experiences
that they had during their careers as professionals or Olym-
pic competitors. Time and time again individual athletes
spoke of the importance of being *in the present* or of feeling
completely at one with a team member or the whole team. All those
interviewed spoke of how important attitude was in everything they did. More than one said, "Attitude is everything,"
that all other things being equal, it was the team that believed
it could win and that did not dwell on its past errors or
failures that won.

On a similar note, O. J. Simpson once told a reporter that
before a play he often had a vivid picture in his mind of the
entire field—his own team as well as the other—unfolding
on the field before him, seconds before it actually occurred.
It was as if he merged so totally with the present that only
the present existed, and he rode that moment like a surfer
on the crescent of a breaking wave, able to foresee exactly
what would occur.

Many professional athletes become so enthusiastic about
sports because it allows them to experience their lives in
ways that are usually available only to people who are highly

disciplined in a spiritual way. Many of our real champions don't look upon opposing team members as enemies but are able to maintain a state of mind that is peaceful, compassionate, and even loving, in the midst of even the toughest competitions.

WALLY HAAS AND THE OAKLAND A'S

I (Jerry) have known Wally Haas since 1970. How he got to be president and chief executive officer of the world-champion Oakland A's (Athletics) baseball team is quite a story. It demonstrates that when you really believe that there are no limitations and that nothing is impossible, what you previously thought impossible becomes a reality.

We have all heard the saying that money does not buy happiness. Those who do not have money often find this statement hard to believe, and there is little question that there are many advantages to coming from a wealthy family. But there are disadvantages too.

One disadvantage of wealth is that it can be difficult to be sure that people like you for yourself and not your money. You may even feel guilty for being lucky enough to come from a family where money is not a problem. Wally Haas's great-great-grandfather had started Levi Strauss & Co. Wally's father, Walter Haas, now retired, was the former president and chairman of the board.

Wally spent time volunteering at the Center, and he was a member of our board for several years. When I first met him, he was working for the Levi Strauss Foundation. Although there were many parts of his work that he enjoyed, he did not see it as his life work.

One day when we were talking, I asked Wally the following question: "If you were to completely forget about what other people might think, and about what you thought was possible or impossible, and I gave you a magic wand so that you could wave it and make a picture of whatever you would like to do, what would that picture look like?"

Wally's face brightened and he smiled, immediately answering, "Ever since I was a little boy, my first love was baseball. I was never a good athlete, but I always had this dream that maybe there was something I could do to be involved with baseball. Of course I always knew it was only a fantasy. If I were to create a picture of exactly what I would like to do, it would be to own and run a baseball team in the Bay Area." He paused and added, "But that would be impossible."

I told Wally, "The only reason it is impossible is because you think it is impossible. If you change your belief system, anything is possible, anything at all." Wally started depreciating himself, saying that he had no experience in this area. "Besides that," he added, "there are no baseball teams for sale in the Bay Area."

"If you really believe in yourself," I said, "there is nothing, absolutely nothing you can't do. And besides, almost everything that is not for sale now may be for sale at the right price in the future. There is no way of knowing for sure what the future will bring."

I remember Wally thinking out loud, saying, "You know, Jerry, my dad loves sports. If something like this could happen, it would bring the two of us much closer together, and we could really get a lot of joy from it."

Well, a month or so passed, and I forgot about our conversation. Then one day Wally told me that he talked with his father about baseball and the idea of having a baseball team. His dad didn't completely negate the idea. In fact he thought the idea had some merit. About two weeks later his father set up a meeting with Bob Lurie, the owner of the San Francisco Giants, and talked to him about the idea of having Wally come into the management division so that he could learn the ropes.

About a week after that, even before Bob Lurie had given him an answer, Wally's father got a phone call from Cornell Maier, then the president of Kaiser Aluminum. Maier told him that Charlie Finley, then the owner of the Oakland A's, was going to sell the team, and there was talk that it would be moved out of Oakland. A week after that Cornell Maier called back again, this time urging Walter to buy the franchise.

After months of negotiations that were as challenging as the most challenging athletic competition, the Haas family became the owners of the Oakland A's. Roy Eisenhardt, Walter's son-in-law, became the president. Wally became executive vice president.

Wally then had a new challenge, to get past his old beliefs in limitations. Part of Wally's job was to build a more positive relationship between the baseball team and the community. This meant that Wally was going to have to give a lot of public speeches, and like most people, the prospect of doing this put him in a panic.

Wally worked hard to change his attitude about himself. He quickly became an excellent speaker and it became something that he thoroughly enjoyed doing.

In 1988 Wally became president of the Oakland A's and finally chief executive officer. As the record books now show, that team won their division and then the American League pennant in 1988, and many times thereafter. In 1989 they even won the World Series.

We were invited to a pregame reception at the World Series, attended by owners and players from many other teams throughout the country. Our memories carried us back to Wally's childhood dream of one day being part of a great baseball team, and we were reminded once again that we truly do live in a limitless world, where dreams really can come true. In order for this to occur, we must first dream and believe in those dreams, then work hard to achieve them, and finally allow them to come true.

WHAT IS ATTITUDE?

Having talked with Wally Haas many times, we knew that he believed that attitude was extremely important. We asked him just how much he felt that attitude had to do with their losing the 1990 World Series four games straight.

Wally replied, "I think attitude had probably everything to do with it. The media had made everyone, including us, believe that we were unbeatable and that we would win in a four-game sweep. On paper the statistics of our performance made us unbeatable. But an *attitude* is something you have to keep in front of your mind at all times.

"We are a team that has functioned best when we are under pressure. We win with our adrenaline running high. As I look back, I think that because we had a period of time to rest, we were not feeling that tight, motivating pressure that we had so many times during the season.

"Now, don't get me wrong; everyone in the club wanted to win. Cincinnati came into the series under great pressure, and we did not. And then our best pitcher, Dave Stewart, lost. That made Cincinnati think that we *were* beatable; and that, at last, put doubts in some of our minds about how invincible we were."

GIVING SOMETHING BACK

For generations the Haas family has upheld a tradition of serving their community and giving something back. That tradition continues with the Oakland A's. Together with Lucky Stores, a supermarket chain in the Bay Area, the Oakland A's build at least one complete baseball field in the community each year. The Bay Area cities of Oakland, Pittsburgh, and Concord have already gotten theirs, and many more are in the planning stages. The Haas family has also created a public-library program to encourage children to read books. They get free and discount tickets to A's games for reading ten or more books.

There are organized intergenerational groups made up of teenagers and older citizens who help out for special events at games. The Haas family has set up a special box with sound equipment so that baseball fans who are visually impaired can enjoy games. And each year the A's make free tickets available to numerous organizations, who distribute them to people who might otherwise not be able to attend games.

The Center for Attitudinal Healing is one of the organizations that receives Oakland A's tickets. We cannot begin to describe how important it is for children with life-threatening illnesses to be out on the ball field shaking hands with their favorite athlete. They experience not only happiness but the fulfillment of their fondest dreams in lives that are often filled with hospitals, pain, and despair.

FORGIVENESS AND LETTING GO OF THE PAST

In the course of managing a large, very popular sports franchise like the Oakland A's, one is reminded again and again of the importance of forgiveness. As the "national pastime," baseball brings Wally and his family into the public eye all the time. There is an endless stream of stories in the media about the team, mostly complimentary but not always. At times there are relationship problems with individual players, too, and the media never seems to miss a thing.

Some of the stories that appear in the media from time to time could certainly be interpreted in a hurtful way. They could easily become the source of much grievance and blame. When we discussed this subject with Wally, he replied, "If you live in the past, if you hold on to grievances and unforgiving thoughts, you are not able to function effectively in the present. Although it isn't always easy, I believe that letting go of the past is an essential process in our day-to-day living, whether at work or at home."

FAMILY SPIRIT

Wally once told us, "I believe that the Oakland A's strive as much or more than any club to have a feeling of family for all our employees, whether they are out on the field or in the office. For example, when we won the World Series, it was customary for just the players to get special rings commemorating their winning. We arranged to have rings made for all the employees of the club. We also have facilities for baby-sitting for all the players' families so that the wives can come to the games. We have done our best to create a feeling of family on and off the field, and I believe that we have been very successful."

WHAT'S IN IT FOR WALLY?

Having heard many stories about the difficulties of running a baseball team, we could not help but wonder what was in it for Wally. It didn't seem to us that it could be easy living on such a roller coaster. Wally answered our questions about this:

"There is something about baseball that goes beyond words. I love the game. I love the atmosphere. I love the smell and the excitement. I love the fact that older people can come out to a game and get away from the challenges that face them daily. I love the fact that it is such a family-oriented game. It gives so many people an outlet to relax, to root for the home team, to yell at the umpire, and to feel that you are watching an extension of yourself.

"I have to tell you that I still find it difficult pacing up and down in the owner's box when our team is losing. It is not easy, by any means, to be living in a fish bowl so much of the time.

"There are a lot of things that are not easy. But they go with the job. Perhaps one of the toughest things to do is to trade a player to another club, especially when it has been someone who has been a member of our team and our family. I guess you learn to take the good with the bad.

"But most of what is in it for me is that our club is in a position to uplift the spirit of Oakland. We are in a position to motivate young people, not just in sports but in their schooling and the other parts of their lives. Take Dave Stewart, our star pitcher, for example. I don't think a day goes by that he is not volunteering his services to someone or some organization. I cannot begin to tell you what a wonderful role model he is for so many. I love baseball because it gives the opportunity to bring about so much joy and joining."

LETTING GO OF THE BELIEF IN LIMITATIONS

When we believe in limitations, they do limit us. When we let go of our belief in limitations, we begin to see new ways of looking at our world. This is as true of physical limitations as it is of psychological or intellectual ones.

In the past few years we have become acquainted with many athletes who have what some would believe to be serious physical handicaps. Yet these physical handicaps are not perceived as limitations by the athletes themselves. There are many one-legged skiers who have mastered the slopes, and in no way do they feel limited or handicapped. There are whole basketball teams of players who play competitively in their wheelchairs, with their games being as exciting and emotional as the most exciting professional teams in the world.

These athletes believe in themselves. They accept their bodies as they are, living completely in the present so that their goal is to do their very best—the same goal that every serious athlete has. They like and love themselves, and there is no room for self-pity because their self-worth is not limited to the body. We will never forget the child at the Center who said, "There is no such thing as handicapped bodies—only handicapped minds." The truth so often comes from the minds of children in such simple but powerful ways.

There are people in their eighties and nineties who continue to play very creditable games of tennis. They run, cycle, and swim. We live near the San Francisco Bay, which is icy cold most of the year. There is a group of people who call themselves the Polar Bear Club who swim there all year-round, even when the weather gets down very close to freezing. They believe that even limitations like one's tolerance for the cold are in one's mind, not one's body.

Angela Dracott

When Angela came to the Center, she really took to creating positive mental images. Her wonderful, creative mind enabled her to let go of her fear and low self-esteem, becoming an inspiration to everyone around her. Her mental pictures were always built on a firm foundation, namely, her desire to make the world a better place to live. She had a commitment to being helpful to others and to believing that nothing was impossible.

Angela came to the Center when she was fifteen years old. She had cystic fibrosis, a disease of the lungs. It is known to be a progressive illness, one that continues to get worse, and it often results in death in the teen years. But Angela continued to thrive.

She became interested in, of all things, fencing. This is a sport that requires incredible stamina and a strong physical and emotional presence. There were many people who felt this was an impossibility for Angela, that she simply didn't have the fortitude the sport called for.

However, Angela was determined. She did not give her power away to others. Her belief structure was unshakable, based on the attitude that nothing is impossible. She believed one hundred percent that what we can do depends on our beliefs.

Not only did Angela become proficient in fencing, she entered many tournaments, up to and including international events, and won many of them!

Angela did not "sort of" believe in herself; her belief was firm and clear. Angela knew that she was not doing things by herself. She said, "I felt I was directed by my inner self— which is God."

Angela is a wonderful example of a person who brings a sense of harmony into body, mind, and spirit. When she enters a room, she brightens the space like a ray of sunlight on a beautiful spring morning.

Tom Quinn

Tom Quinn is a friend of my (Diane's) brother, Andy, who lives in East Quogue, Long Island, in the state of New York. Andy told us about Tom because he had learned so much from Tom about the power we each have within us for overcoming any obstacle, a power that enables us to live joyous and useful lives. Tom lost both legs during the war in Vietnam, yet today he is a great golfer. He is busily engaged in developing tournaments for the physically challenged and has been an inspiration to thousands of men and women who have physical handicaps.

One Saturday morning Tom shared his story as he was going out to play golf. "Before Vietnam," he said, "I was into golf and was the assistant to a golf pro at the club. In Vietnam I walked into a booby trap and lost both legs above the knee. I was bitter and had a terrible time dealing with my situation.

"My self-esteem, who I was, what I could do, was shattered in every way possible. I later got married and did a variety of odd jobs. After about five years my marriage failed, and I am still single."

Recognizing that he was a person who seemed to have an unstoppable spirit, who apparently believed in the power of his heart and his mind, we asked, "When did things change for you? When did you go back to playing golf?"

Tom answered, "I had not played golf for seventeen years after my accident. Then one day I was with a number of older people who were handicapped and confined to wheelchairs. They were very bitter about the past and continued to play the victim role.

"That day I made a declaration to myself. I told myself that the past was gone and that I was no longer going to live in it. I finally told myself that there was no way that I was ever going to be able to change the past. That was the day I picked up a golf club again."

Today Tom plays golf from a wheelchair, and his average tee shot is over two hundred yards. He no longer sees himself as a physically handicapped person, preferring the term *physically challenged* if a term needs to be applied at all. In addition to playing golf he throws javelin, plays basketball, drives a car—performing like a champion in activities that most people who have no physical challenges would never dream of taking on. At the present time he makes his living painting houses, a profession that in itself requires physical strength, agility, and stamina.

We asked Tom, "What is your greatest joy?"

"My biggest joy," he replied, "is helping other people who are physically challenged. For example, every year in Saint Louis there is a one-week camp for young people, ages five to twenty-one, who are physically challenged. I always participate in that.

"Almost all the instructors are in wheelchairs. One instructor teaches tennis, another hockey, another basketball, I teach golf, and it goes on and on. These young people need models so that they can know it can be done. We not only teach them to believe in themselves, we prove to them that, literally, nothing is impossible."

Tom spends much of his time traveling around the country participating in golf tournaments, and he enjoys sponsoring some of them himself.

We asked him, "How do you keep your spirits so high?"

He smiled when he answered this question. "It used to be that having two missing legs dictated how I felt. Now it is my mind that tells me how I feel. Each day I remind myself to be grateful that I have a healthy mind and a body that can do just about anything I want to do. I only think of the positive things I can do and not the negative things I can't."

For anyone interested in getting more information about the activities Tom Quinn has described here, he can be reached at: P.O. Box 377, East Quogue, Long Island, New York 11942. Telephone (516) 653-4226.

Affirmations

1. I will use my active imagination to see myself with no limits of any kind.
2. Whenever I am involved in sports, I will think about cooperation and the ways it might bring more joining and peace.
3. I will use sports as a means of joining with others— with team members, with spectators, and with competitors.
4. Rather than competing with others in order to beat them, I will concentrate on the ways we help each other attain excellence.
5. I will nourish myself today by doing some form of physical exercise.

CHAPTER NINE

❖

Law—Letting Go of Attack and Defense

*Justice of the highest level occurs
when everyone is treated as an equal
and where everyone is
loved and forgiven unconditionally.*

ANOTHER WAY

We seem to be living in a society that reinforces the statement that when something goes wrong in our lives, we should immediately find someone to blame. Are you familiar with that law? There are countless people who have been through divorce, where anger, resentment, guilt, and feelings of having been hurt to the core all too easily get translated into money issues. Sometimes we get engaged in warfare, aimed at hurting each other by competing over who gets what in terms of material possessions, support payments, or custody of the children. Once the battle scene is set, both sides spend many hours, at great legal expense, waging a war where destruction, not compromise, becomes the goal.

Years after a divorce many people look back and see that huge quantities of money spent on lawyers could have been saved if there had been an effort to mediate and heal painful feelings. So many issues could have been resolved if the parties involved had found an alternative to attack-and-defense modes.

LAWSUIT CRAZY

Nearly every day we are being bombarded by television, radio, magazine, and newspaper advertising that encourages us to go to a lawyer immediately if there is any kind of accident, injury, or conflict involving money. The message seems to be that suing someone is the way to go. There seems to be an epidemic of always being on the lookout for ways to get something for nothing, even if it is at the expense of another person.

So many of us are becoming insurance-poor because we

are so fearful that somehow, some way, someone is going to sue us for something. It is as if there is an unidentified enemy out there who is going to jump out at us when we least expect it, so we must protect ourselves in every way we can.

MAYBE . . .

Maybe, just maybe, there is another way to deal with disputes other than by taking each other to court. Certainly there are times in life when injury needs to be addressed, but perhaps there are ways to do this that can be healing rather than only heaping more injury on each other.

Maybe each of us can become determined to find ways of dealing with disagreements so that we do not end up dumping our anger onto others and trying to get revenge. Maybe there is a less costly way to settle our disputes than going to court.

Maybe some of our disputes can be settled even before going to a lawyer. Maybe we can continue to look for settlements that are not hurtful—finding win-win solutions, where both parties gain. Maybe it is possible to listen to each other differently, with a willingness to see all sides of an issue, not just our own.

LAWYERS WHO ARE MAKING A DIFFERENCE

When we are involved in a legal dispute, principles of Attitudinal Healing may seem the farthest thing from our minds. Our first impression may be that the legal system and spiritual issues are such different ways of looking at the world that the two could never be brought together. We may be tempted to believe that it is necessary to have a split mind, telling ourselves that law is just one of those activities where we have to hold on to guilt and blame as our only realities. However, we are beginning to find lawyers throughout the country who are looking at the practice of law in a very different way.

We felt it might be helpful to share with you some of the lessons these lawyers have discussed with us, so that all of us—attorneys as well as people who might be facing difficult legal disputes—might see that it is truly possible to bring into any discussions, no matter how controversial, a sense of peace and joining rather than conflict and separation.

We are finding, even in our own lives, that when faced with issues that require the help of an attorney, it is possible to do so with peace of mind as our only goal. And it is possible to negotiate peaceful solutions even while acknowledging our own anger and the anger of those who might see us as their enemies or adversaries.

In recent years we have had the good fortune of meeting a number of lawyers who are true spirits of innovation in the practice of their professions. These people are looking at their lives and the practice of law and are saying to themselves, "There must be another way of looking at this world than in terms of attack and defense."

These lawyers are taking a whole new look at their belief systems and are in the process of carefully examining every one of their values. They are doing their best to let go of what no longer works for them and to hold on to only those values that do.

Some of these lawyers have been on a spiritual path for years, while others are just beginning their spiritual quest. In their personal lives they are striving to go in the direction of wanting peace of mind as their only goal. It is their intent to live lives without blaming others, making every effort to find their life purpose in being loving, forgiving, and as helpful as they know how to be. They are asking themselves, "Am I here just to make money or am I here to truly help people? Am I living a life of integrity, one that is truly meaningful?"

These lawyers are often finding that the principles governing their personal lives are quite the opposite, or even in direct conflict with, the way they conduct their professional lives. Some have told us that there is a spiritual emptiness practicing in a system that encourages adversarial relationships that emphasize people's separate interests and frequently fan the flames of anger, hate, and vengeance.

ATTITUDINAL HEALING CONFERENCE FOR LAWYERS

Because a number of attorneys requested it, the Center recently held a conference on Attitudinal Healing for lawyers to explore ways to practice law and be helpful to others without practicing attack and defense. It was a fascinating conference, attended by a small number of dedicated lawyers from all over the country. They were seriously interested in finding ways to help create healing solutions as alternatives to the battling of enemy camps that so often sets the tone for legal disputes. The majority of participants felt it was possible to resolve conflicts without dispensing blame and guilt.

CREATIVE SOLUTIONS

Although the exact form for another way of practicing law has only begun to emerge, a different kind of intentionality is becoming clear. Lawyers believe they can begin playing more healing roles, helping to bring about more peaceful solutions to conflicts people are facing. There is a new willingness to find solutions through mediation and negotiation rather than through the courtroom. There is a new desire to create modes of communication that provide the opportunity for creative solutions, rather than depending on attack and defense.

A few lawyers shared with the conference how just listening with unconditional love can be helpful, especially for people in the midst of a divorce. This form of listening allows clients to begin to see that some of the rage and vengeance they experience, which seems so justified, is really directed toward themselves rather than toward the person they were looking upon as their enemy. And it provides a valuable opportunity for people to begin to see all sides of even very difficult situations. This is a very different process than the one in which the belief system of an eye for an eye predominated. There is a very different intentionality here than in the old adversarial approach, in which each person was just trying to gather enough ammunition to destroy the enemy.

LAWYERS WHO ARE FINDING A DIFFERENT WAY

Throughout our travels we have been fortunate to meet a number of lawyers who are on the cutting edge, who are finding more helpful and loving ways of conducting their practices. We would like to share some of their stories with you.

Nancy Veith

We interviewed Nancy Veith, who practices law in California. She told us that she is working hard to incorporate into her law practice some of the Attitudinal Healing principles that she has been discovering on her personal journey in life. For example, she stated that she always tries to remind herself that a vengeful client is a person who is feeling fearful. She elaborated: "I try to perceive a vengeful client as crying out for love rather than allowing myself to conspire with him to express his vengeance in an attempt to alleviate his pain."

She added, "I try to stay in a neutral state and not get caught up in my client's anger or desire to punish someone else. In a sense I see myself as a healer who is practicing law. My intentions are to give my clients a safe environment to express their fears, to see all sides of the issues, to be open-minded, and to look for a solution where both parties win. I focus on finding a workable compromise rather than on waging war and fighting a long, drawn-out, costly, and emotionally draining legal battle that only results in a Pyrrhic victory.

"I suppose another way of saying this is that I try to act as a mediator and an adviser who models integrity and authenticity. I try to speak my truth while remembering that my peace of mind is my primary goal.

"As I think about the practice of law and look at myself and other lawyers, I realize that there have been times when we have not been truly interested in helping other people but have put our own needs and interests first, especially our need to win, to look good, and to feel powerful. We need to be on guard that this does not happen.

"I do find it helpful to meet with like-minded lawyers to explore innovative ways of practicing law that don't encourage attack and defense. In fact one of my deepest longings is to facilitate workshops for attorneys who wish to practice law in a more peaceful way. I enjoyed the Attitudinal Healing conference for attorneys at the Center because I sometimes feel lonely in the legal world. I love to connect with lawyers who have values and beliefs that are similar to mine.

"I believe that more and more lawyers are questioning some of the values in the present ways of practicing law. Intuitively I feel that eventually there will be dramatic changes in the way attorneys practice law. These will bring about healing solutions, not just monetary and punitive solutions."

Phoebe Lauren

In a conversation with Phoebe Lauren, who for many years was the executive director of the Center for Attitudinal Healing, she had the following to say about incorporating Attitudinal Healing principles into the practice of law:

"One of the problems that I see in the present practice of law in regard to divorce is that there is frequently a great effort to gather information to make the other person wrong. There is a great temptation to take the rage and hurt of your client and escalate it in order to win points for her or him.

"I think that there is a role for forgiveness in the divorce process, and the attorney can play an important part in this respect. For example, there are women and men who win their cases in court, perhaps getting a big settlement in terms of money and material possessions, but they still end up lacking inner peace and feeling miserable. They may have believed that they would gain peace of mind when they won their case, but did not realize that their biggest problem was an internal one, an unwillingness to give up their unforgiving thoughts.

"Oftentimes clients do not understand that it is their own unforgiving thoughts about themselves, being projected onto their spouses, that are causing their distress. I feel that the lawyer can play a role in this forgiveness process, but at times I think it is necessary to refer clients for psychotherapy in order to work on this problem."

We asked Phoebe if she could tell us about a recent example where she had applied Attitudinal Healing principles in her own practice. She replied, "I was involved in a custody suit where there were about six issues of disagreement. As I was working with my client, I remembered that one of the principles at the Center is 'This instant is the only time there is.'

"I did my best to keep the couple focused on what was happening now, rather than on their fear of the past or of the future. One of the issues was who was going to pay for the child's college education.

"By concentrating on the present, they both agreed that the ex-husband was already taking care of all the financial needs that had been asked for and that both parties really had clarity about both of their desire to be helpful in the higher-education process. When there was a willingness of both parties to let go of the fears of the past, which were being projected onto the future, and to concentrate just on the present, all six issues were agreed to with harmony, in a relatively short period of time. I feel that the lawyer can play a role in helping the client to let go of the attachments, hurts, and fears of the past and future.

"Another principle at the Center is 'Everyone is an equal

teacher to each other.' I do my best to establish a relationship where I am a consultant and co-worker with my client, and I am focused on establishing a relationship of equality. This means I don't play the dominant role, and I don't make decisions for my client. Full empowerment is given for my clients to make all decisions after working together jointly. I don't foster disabling dependent feelings.

"Because I have seen so much law practiced in a mode of anger and attack, which so often ends up with serious repercussions to clients, I work very hard at not practicing law by being on a 'head trip'; I do my best not to let any blockage occur between my heart and my head and between my heart and my client's heart.''

Judge James McNalley

Attorneys are not the only ones who have begun bringing the principles of Attitudinal Healing into the courtroom setting. We have been very privileged to know at least one judge who is doing everything he can to create a courtroom setting where creative solutions can be found.

James McNalley has been a superior-court judge in Ventura, California, for over ten years. He is a student of the principles of Attitudinal Healing and makes every effort to live them to the fullest in both his personal and his professional life. Other judges, as well as attorneys, have described his courtroom as one of the most peaceful they have ever been in.

Judge McNalley told us, "It is my job to make decisions but it is not my job to hurt people. In making decisions I do my best to determine who is responsible. I find many people in my court who are very fearful, regardless of which side of the table they may be on. I feel that it is very helpful for me to see people as fearful rather than as being uncaring, mean, or whatever other negative words we might want to use when a person is being difficult. I am not known as an easy judge . . . but I do have a reputation for being a fair one.

"It is my job to make decisions based on the law. It doesn't mean that I don't care about people or don't recognize the environmental factors that may have contributed to a particular offense. My job is to protect society in as fair and humane a way as I know how. It is not always easy.

"I think that love and caring can be brought into the courtroom by the judge. It is hard, sometimes, when it is such an adversarial environment."

Sara Maurer

Sara is a volunteer at the Center and has a private law practice in San Francisco. She described for us some of her experiences in the practice of law:

"My first ten years as a lawyer I practiced real estate law for big corporate firms in New York City and Boston. I made tons of money, but I ended up feeling spiritually empty. I was making money for companies and myself, but I was not really contributing in a meaningful way to the world. And that was one of the reasons I wanted to become a lawyer—to deal with injustice in a helpful and meaningful way. I am now in private practice and I feel I have a heart-to-heart connection with people as I do my best to assist them."

We asked Sara to tell us a little about how she applied the principles of Attitudinal Healing in her practice. She replied, "Just the other day my partner had a terrible fight with another lawyer on the phone, and he hung up on her. After my partner cooled down, he asked me if I would call and try to heal things. I said that I would try. I called up the other lawyer, who was so angry at my partner, she yelled and hung up on me.

"I did my best to be defenseless and chose not to believe that I was attacked. I remembered that one of the principles at the Center is that 'This is the only time there is.' The next day I decided to let go of the past. I again called the lawyer who had yelled at me and said to her, 'It is a new day. I am willing to let go of yesterday and I hope that you might be too. Can we start over?' I received a positive response, and an agreement was made for a settlement outside of court.

"Another example I remember is when a city attorney told me that I was inexperienced and would certainly lose a particular case if I went to court. My ego got the best of me. I became angry and hung up. The next day, to my surprise, she called back and asked me for a favor, to extend the time on the case. I was able to choose to see her reactions of the previous day as being due to fear, so I had no problem granting her request. In the past I would probably have wanted to get even with her, to have my revenge, and would have said no.

"Still another example of not making judgments of other people is a situation in which I was representing parents of a teenager who was run over by a train. At the deposition of the woman who had been the driver of the train, I could see and feel her anguish. Although I felt she was responsible, I felt no need to judge her with guilt and blame. I do think there is a difference between guilt feelings and being responsible. Another way of saying this is that I am learning to be empathetic and understanding of everyone who is involved in any case I am working on."

Gary Friedman

We were told by several people that an attorney by the name of Gary Friedman had been very successful at incorporating spiritual principles into his practice and that he was gaining tremendous personal fulfillment, as well as being professionally successful, in doing so. We asked Gary to tell us his story.

"From 1970 until 1975 I worked in a firm that had been started by my father and my uncle," he said. "I did criminal and civil litigation, spending a good deal of time in court, which at first I found quite exciting. After the first several years I began to look at myself and noticed that although I was seen as a successful lawyer, there was something missing inside. Almost everything in the courtroom was involved in using my head. While that had its place, particularly in terms of the classic role of protecting one's client and maximizing his or her interests, and I could do it well, I became increasingly aware that there were no heart connections.

"Litigation practice was set up in such a way that not only

were you protecting your client but you were also protecting yourself from all areas of vulnerability. Being careful was at a premium, caring was not. There seemed to be little place for honest, spontaneous feelings and thoughts outside those narrowly defined by roles. I began to have feelings that I was not supposed to have. For example, after winning a case I would look at the face of the person who had just lost and feel empathy for that individual. He, she, or they were not just objects.

"I did not feel balanced in my personal or professional life. I decided that there had to be another way of living and another way of practicing law. I dropped out of practice and began doing some self-exploratory work. I met another lawyer with similar interests, and together we obtained a grant from the National Institute of Mental Health for training law professors in humanistic educational approaches to understanding professional roles. I soon found myself opening up a practice specializing in mediation."

We asked Gary to tell us a little about his spiritual pathway. He replied, "I have become very involved in the Buddhist philosophy. I was raised in the Jewish faith, and I guess I could be called a Jewish Buddhist." He began describing some of the ways he had brought his beliefs into his law practice: "I do my best to be true to myself in both my personal life and my legal practice. Whereas I was previously caught up in the system of being confrontational and competitive, I now find that I am going in the opposite direction. I work from the premise that one person is not right and the other wrong but that there is truth and fault on both sides. My job is to help people find solutions, without having to be steeped in shame, blame, and guilt—to help them find a space where they can still protect themselves but at the same time strive toward mutual understanding in the effort to reach agreement.

"Rather than attempting to find solutions based exclusively on my intellect, I now include an awareness of other dimensions of experience—both mine and those of the people I work with. I am involved with and am on the board of directors at the Zen Meditation Center, and I find that meditation is a tremendous help for bringing me a sense of balance, helping me to be in touch with my intuitive self.

"Perhaps the most important difference in me today, in contrast to how I was when I started my practice twenty years ago, is that I now have a practice that has *heart-to-heart* connections. That seems essential, not just personally but professionally—in terms of serving the parties who come to me for legal assistance. As a litigator I am not so sure how really helpful I was to people. While I was very successful at *winning* cases, I seemed to follow the unwritten law of covering up and protecting our hearts. I now feel that it is not only okay but it is critically important to allow oneself to be vulnerable and to feel one's connections with others— not as a substitute for analytical thinking but as an indispensable complement."

We asked Gary what it was that he saw as his life purpose. He answered that while that is always evolving, it continues to have to do with his *connection with others*. In addition to his law practice at Mediation Law Offices in Mill Valley, he is actively involved in training lawyers in this country and Europe in the approach to mediation that he has been developing—an approach that emphasizes the importance of human understanding.

It was so clear to us that Gary is living a fulfilled life. He is seeking a life of authenticity, one in which he can honestly say that he can strive to be true to himself in his practice of law and in his personal life. It has seemed to us that he has learned not to live a life that has separate compartments; he is living one life, holding his principles of giving, helping, and loving close to his heart wherever he is.

Susan Passovoy

Susan Passovoy has been practicing real estate law for over twenty years. She is on her own spiritual path and is a student of *A Course in Miracles*. Although it is not always easy, Susan tries to apply spiritual principles in both her business and her personal life. One of the principles that has been most helpful to her is the one about experiencing others as either loving or giving a call for help. She said, "When I feel an adrenaline rush after it seems that someone has attacked me, I try to see that person differently. I then remind myself that this person doesn't feel safe or he would not be behaving that way.

"I remind myself that the person who seems to be attacking me is fearful. Then I say a little prayer and ask for help in forgiving him, with the desire to create a safe place for him. I then find my adrenaline going down and I start to feel more peaceful. I find the forgiveness process very practical because it puts me in a neutral situation, both at work and in my personal life. I am learning that it is not other people who upset me. It is only my own thoughts and attitudes about them that cause me distress."

THE LAWYERS' CLIENTS

When we are in need of a lawyer, we may find many temptations to make judgments not just about the person we are facing in the litigation process but about the lawyers themselves. Our phone calls may not be returned or our lawyer may not have kept an agreement to do his or her homework by a certain appointed date.

It is certainly not easy to keep our peace of mind when there are so many judgments being made and where there may be an atmosphere of anger and attack all the time. And it can certainly be easy to lose your peace of mind when you receive your lawyer's bill and find out how large it is.

Many of us who have gone through divorces may recall the bitterness and anger we experienced and how it did not go away just because the litigation had ended. Perhaps we chose to blame the lawyers, to complain that if they had done their jobs a little differently, we would be feeling more peacefulness inside ourselves. When the final outcome is not to our liking, it is particularly easy to find ourselves seeking someone to blame, instead of seeing that it is really our own thoughts and feelings that are causing us to feel upset.

So many times, when we seek the services of a lawyer, we are fearful and feel that we cannot make our own decisions where the law is concerned. We then give our power away, asking them to make decisions that are our own responsibility. It is up to us as clients to perhaps look upon our attorneys not as final authorities but as consultants whose knowledge can assist us in making these difficult choices.

We can remind ourselves that whenever we encounter attack thoughts, whether our own or other people's, we can see them as expressions of being fearful and giving a cry of help for love.

We can remind ourselves that in our defenselessness our safety lies. We can also remind ourselves to seek mediation and negotiation rather than choosing up sides and holding on to an adversarial role. We can remind ourselves that mediation often starts by going inside ourselves and asking how the present situation can be a teacher to us, mirroring back a part of ourselves that it is time to forgive and heal.

As clients we need to take another look at our goals. Many of us go into battle with the goal of winning at any cost and the thought that beating the other person down is the only thing that will bring us peace of mind. Yet all too often the act of winning doesn't bring us that peace we so desire. On the contrary, it leaves us weary and battle-scarred. Too often our anger and bitterness continue because we did not realize that peace of mind has nothing to do with winning. We need constantly to remind ourselves that peace of mind has nothing to do with the outside. It has to do with our own thoughts and feelings and our willingness to let go of guilt, anger, and revenge.

THERE IS ANOTHER WAY OF LOOKING AT LAW

The following is a compilation of suggestions offered by lawyers who are successfully using Attitudinal Healing in their law practices. These suggestions are offered for those who want to find a way of practicing law other than attack and defense. The same suggestions can be helpful for clients.

1. *Remind* yourself that your role is one of mediator, negotiator, and healer.

2. *See* all your clients, as well as other attorneys, as fearful whenever they appear to be defensive or attacking.

3. *Listen* to your clients' fears, but don't join their insanity by becoming an extension of their desire for vengeance.

4. *Be clear* about your own boundaries so that you don't need to defend and protect yourself.

5. *Create* a support system for yourself, perhaps with other lawyers who are also looking for another way.

6. *Be open* to suggesting therapeutic counseling, if appropriate, for clients harboring anger, rage, and pain. Winning the case alone does not make these feelings go away.

7. *Direct* clients toward what can concretely be agreed upon today rather than toward what may or may not occur in the future.

8. *Be a co-worker* with your client as well as a consultant. This will leave much more room for creative solutions.

9. *Foster independence* rather than dependence in your clients, and the healing process will be enhanced.

10. *Empower your clients* to ultimately make their own decisions.

11. *Keep the road open* between your own heart and head to demonstrate that it is possible for others.

12. *Promote* an environment, both physically and psychologically, for you and your client that is peaceful and caring.

13. *Represent* your client in the fairest and most humane way possible.

14. *Focus your quest* for information objectively instead of building mountains of blame and guilt.

15. *Find ways to join* clients rather than separate them.

16. *Ask* yourself periodically if your present area of law is bringing you the satisfaction, growth, and happiness you seek.

17. *Choose each day* to let go of previous grievances through forgiveness in order to make way for new choices in life.

18. *Identify clearly* the difference between guilt and responsibility, since you will promote one or the other, depending on what you hold in your mind.

19. *Extend* love instead of fear in your practice.

20. *Remind* yourself each day that living both your personal and your professional life with harmony and continuity will bring you the peace of mind you deserve.

❖

CHAPTER TEN

Prejudice and Discrimination

*All prejudice and discrimination
is reversible
because all of it comes from fear.*

ATTITUDES THAT KILL

As we write this chapter, it seems that in the world there is a growing escalation of prejudice and discrimination. And there is an increased awareness that attitudes such as these affect all of us, even when we are not, at this moment, the actual recipient or perpetrator.

Whenever prejudice and discrimination occur, we are not able to see each other as we really are. Oppression can take many different forms. It can occur in our childhoods when other children make fun of us because we are not as good at sports as the rest of them. It can occur because we are from a different racial, religious, or ethnic background than most of the others in the neighborhood where we live or attend school.

If you have ever been oppressed, if you or your family has been on the receiving end of an attack of any kind, if you have witnessed a senseless killing, have seen your home or business destroyed, or have been refused employment because of race, creed, or sex, or if you have been refused the right to live in a certain neighborhood, then you know what fear is all about.

You also know how it feels to experience the vicious cycle of "justified" anger, which leaves us feeling emotionally depleted, fearful, and lacking in peace.

For so many people who come from Jewish backgrounds there is a growing fear that anti-Semitism is on the rise again throughout the world. In many people's minds these fears revive memories of the dark shadows of Auschwitz and the Holocaust. Clearly the expressions of prejudice are continuing to grow throughout the world.

If you are black you may feel very dissatisfied with the lack of equal justice, as well as educational and job opportunities that are available to you, compared with what is available to the white population.

As an Hispanic, Asian, or other minority, opportunities are often available only with great struggle. If you are a lesbian or gay person, you know the pain of being different from the mainstream. If you have AIDS, you may have suffered rejection, not only by your church, your community, your health-care worker, and the people in your workplace but also by your own family.

Discrimination against women in the workplace continues to be a major source of injustice in every country in the world, in spite of the fact that women constitute more than half the world's population. The small number of women in influential positions throughout the world has more to do with the discriminatory practices of men than it does with the competency of women. Likewise, discrepancies in equal pay for equal work continue to challenge many.

There is a great temptation throughout the world for one minority group to make another minority group the target of their own fears and prejudices. We see this in virtually every community where there are people who suffer discrimination at the hands of the majority.

No matter what our walk in life, we can easily fall into the trap of believing that there is no problem with our own thinking, logic, or actions. We can find all kinds of "reasons" and "proofs" to justify our prejudices.

A GLOBAL RESPONSIBILITY

Although you may not have suffered discrimination because of your identification with a particular minority, there is probably no one alive who has not been either the recipient or the perpetrator of prejudice and discrimination at some time in his or her life. It is commonplace to point the finger at others, but the reality is that eliminating these attitudes that kill is a global job that begins and ends with each one of us.

The flame of prejudice has been the source of incredible human suffering for centuries. It has caused wars and bloodshed far too vast to recount. And almost always these wars have been fought in the name of God. The resulting feelings of righteousness and indignation, often shared by entire nations, have fostered illusions of separation that are cast in stone, lasting for many, many generations. The roots of prejudice and discrimination are always the same: fear and guilt, projected out onto others. Find a person who feels totally loved by the universe, who experiences himself or herself as love, who has faith and trust in love, who believes that there is another way of living in this world than by attacking each other, and you will find a person who is devoid of prejudice and discrimination.

FEAR AND GUILT

A part of each of us is always on the alert to find an enemy, that is, a person or event that is to blame for the fear we are experiencing. From that standpoint, what better enemy than one who appears to be weaker and more vulnerable, is smaller in numbers, speaks a different language, looks different, or is of another sex?

Perpetrators of hate and violence, prejudice and discrimination, are usually themselves suffering from feelings of guilt, weakness and vulnerability, and feelings of being victimized. Although they camouflage their inner feelings behind words and deeds that make them seem superior or stronger, the pain and suffering are nevertheless there.

When we look closely at these people's lives, we often find personal histories of having been attacked, sexually abused, emotionally or physically violated, or discriminated against in a way that was quite hurtful. Their rage, resentment, and feelings of revenge are then projected outward, finding targets in other people, usually ones that are weaker or at least more vulnerable than themselves.

DENIAL AND REPRESSION OF FEELINGS

The attitudes we so frequently see in those who are most outspoken in their prejudice are ones of arrogance and self-righteousness, imbued with a lack of willingness to examine their own belief systems. Their beliefs are often associated with a long history of repression, abuse, deprivation, and denial—all of which make the feelings, buried so deeply within themselves, very threatening and fearful.

When you have experienced not just years but centuries of hardship, oppression, belittlement, cruelty, and the death of relatives and loved ones, the need to feel strong and dominant rises from within you, driven by an overwhelming need to survive at any cost. When these attitudes are dominant in our lives, we are tempted to unite with others like ourselves, through what seems to be our justified anger, hatred, and desire for revenge. Together we fabricate an illusion of strength and safety by finding a common enemy to become the target of our attack thoughts—which are all too often expressed in real acts of oppression.

EQUALITY

One of the most important principles at the Center for Attitudinal Healing is that everyone is equally a student and a teacher to each other. As we look closely at attitudes of prejudice and discrimination, it is important to be reminded that love knows only equality and joining. On the opposite end of the scale, fear, blame, and guilt only know separation and inequality. Although it is not easy to see how our oppressors—who seem so willing to create separation—could possibly be teachers to us, it is often through choosing to see them in this way that we find peace within ourselves.

If we are the oppressed, there have undoubtedly been

times when we ourselves were tempted to oppress others, thereby walking in the same shoes as those who would oppress us. By looking at our oppressors as mirror images of unhealed aspects of ourselves, we can begin to change our attitudes about ourselves and others. It is not always easy to do this. If we have experienced oppression, if we have had others treat us as second-class citizens, it can be very difficult for us to imagine that equality and inner peace could ever be a reality. But we need not be limited to our perceptions of what's possible. When we have the willingness to believe that it is possible, we find there really is another way of looking at the world.

To free ourselves of prejudice and discrimination, it is essential to remember that these emotions are not carved in stone, nor can they imprison us in the role of victim forever. We can choose to no longer find any value, positive or negative, in any of the attitudes about oppression that we might presently be holding in our minds. We can let them go no matter how justified they may seem to be.

LESSONS OF THE HOLOCAUST

One of the most important learning experiences of my (Jerry's) life was working for three years with people who were children during the Holocaust. Many of them were prisoners in concentration camps and experienced cruelties beyond my comprehension, abuses that seem completely unforgivable. Yet these same people who had suffered such unbelievable horror and hardship taught me that there is always another way of looking at the world, and sometimes it takes great personal courage to find it. Although I was there trying to do my part to help them, there was another part of me that found it difficult to imagine how they could even have survived such hardships.

The members of our Holocaust group never really experienced being children. They were separated from their parents and families when they were still very young and vulnerable. Surrounded each day by incredible cruelty and the constant presence of death, most of them felt that the only possible way to survive was to trust no one. Hunger, cold, fear, and pain often seemed to be their only reality. Why? What had they done? They were there for only one reason—they were Jewish.

All the members of our Holocaust group, having survived the ordeal of their imprisonment, went on to become very successful in their businesses and professions. Some, however, were still ruled by fears learned early in their lives. Their sleep was often disturbed by nightmares about the things they had witnessed in the past. Others had let go of the past to a large extent and were living lives that were full of love and very little fear.

One woman in our group had much to teach all of us about overcoming the fear and bitterness anyone might be tempted to hold on to as a result of the ways he or his loved ones were treated. This woman told how she had escaped death when she was a child in the camp. An older person had stuffed her into the middle of a pile of dead bodies that was being removed. Much later in her life, after she had come to the United States, she was working at Napa State Hospital, in California. It was there that she had a transformational experience that helped her to see her experiences at Dachau in a new way.

She was assigned to work with chronic schizophrenic patients while doing an internship in the back wards. Many of these people had been in catatonic states for years. She said, "As I came into that ward, I could immediately see how fearful each of the patients was. They were looking at me as if I was their jailer. I felt a question being raised within me: 'Who is the jailer, and who is the jailed?' And I wondered, were my jailers also victims during the war?

"Somehow that day I felt the palpable presence of God in a way that I never had before. I knew that to be truly alive, I had to let go of my attachment to that horrendous past and forgive. I knew that my life's work was then going to be helping others, through love and forgiveness. My life has not been the same since that day. Now I find that when I am concentrating on living in the present, I don't think about the past. And when I concentrate on helping others, I feel less helpless myself!"

Another person in our group, Dr. John Michael Steiner, who is a professor at a local university, began going back to Germany to interview some of the people who had been his jailers or had been responsible for the death camps. Although he originally went back with animosity in his heart, something very strange happened to him during his visits. As he got to know each of the men better, he began to see them as prisoners of their own lives.

Out of his experiences he became convinced that as long as we are attached to being victims and holding grudges, we are doomed to be imprisoned by the pain of the past. He now believes, with all his heart, that each of us is capable of letting go of the past, living in the present, and preparing for the future. We can do this by understanding, helping, loving, and forgiving. No matter what the severity of pain and injustice we have experienced, we can be transformed from our past grievances if we have a willingness to change our attitudes.

THE POWER OF THE HUMAN SPIRIT

There is a spirit within every human heart that never gives up hope, burning like an eternal flame. In 1990 the world was witness to this as the Iron Curtain at last came down, changing the face of Europe. We see further proof of its presence each time another group, somewhere in the world, breaks free of the oppression that once held them.

Somehow the razing of the Iron Curtain has become the symbol of the indomitable human spirit for the whole world. The removal of that wall seems to represent a sense of joining and oneness for people everywhere. It doesn't seem to us that the wall's coming down was solely the result of political action. It came down because there were so many people who wanted a way of life that allowed them the freedom and power to be who they are.

There are many people, ourselves included, who believe that what really brought the wall down was the indomitable spirit within each oppressed person in the region that made the difference. It has been a powerful lesson for all of us, the world over, reminding us that the transformation of the individual transforms society.

TEACHERS OF PEACE IN BELFAST

On our visits to Belfast we found the bitterness and hatred between Catholics and Protestants permeating every aspect of society. We heard horror stories about the terrible loss of life and the destruction of property, of innocent people becoming victims of bombings and shootings. Buildings and entire neighborhoods had been destroyed, with nothing left but piles of debris to mark the spot where they had been. Soldiers patrolled the streets while children threw rocks at them. On some streets fences separated Catholic from Protestant housing.

We were visiting a family with nine children, the father of whom had recently died of cancer. During our visit we were told that just a week ago two soldiers had been killed by a bomb directly across the street from where this family lived and that this was a relatively common occurrence.

Many families had undergone years of economic as well as emotional hardship. One neighborhood we visited had 90 percent unemployment. In this environment children grew up experiencing a great deal of fear and hatred from the first days of their lives. You could almost taste anger and despair in the air, and it felt that at any moment a spark of conflict was going to ignite it. It was as if gasoline had been poured over the whole area and it could suddenly explode into flames.

Months later I (Jerry) was in the Middle East with my friend Dr. Landrum Bolling. We visited Jordan, the Left Bank, and the Gaza Strip. The flames of anger and hatred seemed no different here than they had in Ireland. Only the names and forms were different.

A CHANGE OF MIND, A CHANGE OF LIFE

After visiting so many places in the world where bitterness, turmoil, killing, and destruction had been a way of life for generations, it is difficult even to imagine viable solutions or to find reason for hope. And yet we came away more than ever convinced that one person can and does make a difference in the world and that the light each one of us can shine goes a long, long way.

In Belfast we met one such light, a man of boundless courage and hope. We believe that he is an inspiring example of what can happen when just one person decides that there has to be another way of finding social justice than through attack and defense. This was a man who was willing to make a break with old systems and to see the world differently.

Just meeting this man and hearing his story gave us both a lot of hope. He was in his late twenties and he was totally blind. He had recently opened up an after-school recreational area that brought together Protestant and Catholic children. People told him that he was crazy for even trying this, that parents would not dare let their children mix with those from "the other side."

There was plenty of apprehension at first, but the worst fears of the man's friends turned out to be wrong. A few Protestant and Catholic families began sending their kids to him. At first the children didn't know quite what to expect. It was as if they thought they would find horns growing out of each other's head. Obviously they all discovered this wasn't the case, and as they continued playing together, a miracle happened; they discovered that they actually liked each other. As time went on and the word got out that the children were actually making friends, more children began showing up. The beauty was that now they had their own experiences to build on. They were no longer depending on old beliefs and prejudices to make choices about who were to be their friends.

There was no magic here. Perhaps the most important thing that happened was really something that was very, very simple. The children were treated as equals, and unconditional love was given to all. There was no categorization of people, no identification of them as enemies or friends based on their religious background.

As time went on, the children began sharing their experiences with their parents. Soon children were phoning each other. Then they began visiting in each other's home. As this began happening more and more, families not only met, they became friends, no longer limited by the centuries-old boundaries they had inherited.

We asked our new friend how he happened to start this project. He said that he was a Protestant and that at the age of fifteen a bomb went off in front of his house. He had been outside playing when it happened and was permanently blinded.

He went on to say, "I know this might surprise you, but in one way being blinded finally *opened me eyes* to see! I had a real awakening. I began to see that what was important in me was spiritual vision, not visual acuity.

"I began to believe that each of us can make a difference and that the buck had to stop somewhere, so why not with me? I consciously chose not to be a victim. I decided not to live the rest of my life with hatred and vengeance, as I saw so many others around me doing.

"God came into my life in a very real way," he continued. "I found how important forgiveness was in my life. I found that it was actually possible to forgive the people who had blinded me, as well as to forgive myself for the things that I had done.

"It was then that I felt I had received some guidance from heaven to start this small, after-hours school and not to worry about the negative advice of others. My job was clearly to treat everyone as equals and to love everyone unconditionally. I am absolutely delighted that in a small way I am making a contribution. And I know that I will never give up hope."

Afterward this man invited us over to his tiny apartment. While there he showed us a trophy he had won for the best photograph taken by a blind person. To us that trophy was for a lot more than taking a photograph. It was a trophy of recognition that here was a man who not only believed that nothing was impossible but proved it through his actions every day of his life. There could be no doubt that this was a man who had total trust and faith.

Aeesha Ababio

Aeesha Ababio is a remarkable woman who heads the West Oakland Attitudinal Healing Center in Oakland, California. Aeesha has been a dear friend for many years. A former Black Muslim, she has done wonders incorporating Attitudinal Healing principles into her personal and professional lives. She works as a social worker at a halfway house for people who are mentally challenged.

As we were writing this chapter, we asked her for some advice and for examples of what she had been doing to deal with prejudice in her own life. Her response to our request had much to teach everyone who has ever struggled with this issue.

Aeehsa told us that for many years she was a political activist, fighting against social injustice. She would yell, scream, march, and even take people to court. And then one day she made a decision. She decided that there was enough hate and anger in the world, and she was not going to perpetuate it any further.

Rather than continuing to see others as attacking her, she began to change her perception and see them as fearful. She said it was not easy at first, but she was determined to do it. She went on to tell us the following story:

"I was with my daughter, Amana, and we dropped by a Chinese take-out restaurant in a neighborhood where I had never been before. We ordered rice and prawns. We waited about ten minutes and didn't get served. I noticed other people who came in after us getting served.

"So I went up to the lady and asked what had happened, and she didn't say anything. She just left. Five minutes later she came back and I asked again, and she replied, 'We don't serve your kind.'

"Well, in the past that would have been enough to set me into a rage, and I would have threatened, in no uncertain terms, to sue them. Somehow that day I was able to keep my cool by really seeing this person as fearful.

"I was quite prepared to leave peacefully, and when she returned, I told her, 'You know, it is perfectly okay for you not to serve me. Maybe it is the policy here, or maybe you have had a bad experience with someone in the past. But I just wanted to remind you that I didn't do anything to hurt you.' After saying that we started to leave.

"Then I heard a gentle voice call out, 'Please come back. I made a mistake. I'm sorry. I'll serve you.'"

Aeesha went on to say that she is finding that Attitudinal Healing principles really have practical applications in her life. She said that as she has learned to change her perception and to see people either as loving or as fearful, giving a call of help for love, she has had more peace in her life than ever before. She is convinced that by her putting an end to her own justified anger, she has allowed people around her to make new choices to change also.

ELEVEN-YEAR-OLDS CAN MAKE DECISIONS

We have so much to learn about the indomitable spirit of hope that lives in all of us, expressing itself and shining its beacon of light even from the darkest corners. An eleven-year-old girl from a rough, drug-ridden tenement project in Chicago who recently lost her mother in a violent encounter is just such a beacon. Both her father and her brother had been killed in other unrelated killings, and yet her light continues to shine as brightly as the brightest.

Through all the trauma and pain, which will probably take years for this girl even to begin to resolve, this orphaned child, now living with her grandmother, has stated with absolute, clear determination, "I am going to change my life. I am going to make something out of my life and then, someday, after I leave this project, I am going to come back to try to prevent other kids from having to go through what I did. I can do it and I will."

The adversities of life can be cruel teachers. Yet, as this young "teacher" shows us, we can choose at any moment in time to change the course of our lives by shifting our perceptions, by looking at our lives from a slightly different perspective.

What makes the difference in how we choose to approach new ideas, the future, or the way we learn? It is easy to say that we are just products of our environment, our family's values, our education, peer pressure, and other social pressures. However, in the search to find another way of looking at the world, it is helpful to remember that even though these factors helped shape our lives in the past, they need not dictate the choices we make in the present.

EACH OF US HAS CHOICES

Each of us has many choices, and each moment of our lives we can choose once again. We do not have to remain victims of our environment. However, to find another way we have to do much work to not give knee-jerk responses that are based on our past experiences and conditioning.

We can choose to look inside ourselves each day, to see if there are any residues of fear, judgment, anger, and hate. If we do find them, we can choose to see the value of changing our minds, letting go of our negative and judgmental thoughts. These new choices are what change our lives. We can choose at any time to make up our minds to create a present that is not determined by the dark shadows of the fearful and hurtful past. We can choose a present that is based on love and forgiveness.

We can remind ourselves that peace of mind will only become a reality as we neutralize our negative judgments of each other and believe in equality with all our hearts. Peace of mind will not be ours until we have the same interest in others that we have in ourselves.

When we continue to see each other's lights, the power of the miracle of love comes into our lives. When that happens, when we begin to change our minds, our lives will change also, and prejudice and discrimination will begin to vanish from the earth.

Affirmations

1. Today I will see everyone as equal.
2. If I find myself judging others, I will remind myself that it is because in some way I am judging myself.
3. When I hate others, it is because in some way I hate myself.
4. When I am mean to others, it may be because I have not healed my past where others were mean to me.
5. If I feel a sense of righteousness toward others, it may be because I am trying to make someone else wrong in order to make myself right.

❖

THE HEALING OF ATTITUDES IN BUSINESS—PART I

*Perhaps the most important business
of any day is caring,
loving, and being of service to others.*

The World of Business Affects All of Us

Even if we don't think of ourselves as business people, we nevertheless engage in the activity of business every time we go into a store for groceries, a book, or a tube of toothpaste; purchase gasoline for our cars or buy a gift for a friend; send in a check for our utility bill or rent or buy a home; or any of a million and one other activities of this kind.

So much of the time we find that our business relationships are anything but peaceful. We may feel that if we are not constantly on our guard, the other person will take advantage of us. When we do this we experience a sense of separation between ourselves and others, as if the sales counter between us was a battle line that neither of us should ever cross over.

For many of us the mere mention of the word *business* seems to cause us to forget about our spiritual identity. Our egos tell us that where the business world is concerned, we must always be fearful rather than loving and be ready to attack and defend at every turn. Just as with law and the courts, we may feel that we are in an adversarial environment where we are in danger of becoming victims.

In business transactions, when we are on the customer side of the counter, there are many times that we may feel a sense of frustration—when the price of gasoline goes up, when we think that a clerk in the department store has been rude to us, or when we think the president of a large corporation or its board of directors is not doing their part to keep the environment clean. At these times particularly we may feel a sense of separation between the business person and ourselves.

Even though it may seem that we must have split minds and that we must keep our business and spiritual lives completely separate, the fact remains that the transformation of our attitudes and values in business is already taking place. Whether we are a part of the corporate structure, an employee, or a customer, we all have an opportunity to play an important part in this transformation.

Since so much of everybody's time is involved in some aspect of business, we shall explore some of the issues that may cause conflict, as well as some of the possible solutions.

UNFOLDING A NEW VISION

As we approach the new millennium, there is growing evidence that business leaders will be playing essential roles in discovering new ways to relate to the world and to each other that take our spirituality into account. The numbers are not yet great, but this trend is already becoming evident, a fact that is explored in John Naisbitt's and Patricia Auberdine's excellent best-seller *Megatrends 2000*.

Especially in those businesses where competition is the name of the game, there are feelings of fear, anger, and blame, just as there are in the many other areas of our lives. These feelings can cause a very troubling sense of separation. More than ever before, business organizations, and many labor organizations that work with them, and even those of us who are customers, are in powerful positions at this time in history to make a difference in how we communicate with one another. The values and attitudes on both sides of the sales counter are undergoing vast changes.

Perhaps the best way to begin to share with you the many ways in which Attitudinal Healing can come into the business arena is to tell you the stories of real people in real businesses who are already making these changes. Some of these businesses are big, some small. But they are all attempting to find a more humane and caring way to conduct business.

These business people are making important contributions toward healing many of the stereotypes and sources of fear and pain that have for so long created a sense of separation, not only between management and workers but between the businesses and the rest of us who buy products and services.

These are people like you and me who are concerned about doing what may well be the most important thing any of us can do—in every area of our lives—which is to bring about more joining and less separation. These individuals and companies are making a difference and demonstrating that there truly is another way of looking at the world, and business is no exception.

Most of the people in these stories would be the first to admit that they are not always on target and that if healthy growth is to take place, we must be willing to risk making a few mistakes along the way. So many of our most creative solutions come about when we have a willingness to learn from our mistakes and continue to look forward to the future with hope and optimism.

"Love Is the Essence of Our Being"[1]

Sue Siegel is one person who is truly making a difference in the business world. Sue is on her own personal, quiet spiritual journey. She has had a very traumatic past, but rather than be bitter she has chosen to learn from those experiences. She has helped to create a company where people are not objects and where it is okay to talk about feelings.

As a person who has done much to create a caring attitude for both her employees and her customers, we thought it would be worthwhile to go into Sue's past in some detail.

Sue Siegel started manufacturing women's clothes in 1967, and established her company under the name of Sue J. Inc. The clothes they make are known under the brand name Joan Walters.

Out of its very small beginning Sue J. Inc. has expanded to over seventy-five employees and does a multimillion-dollar business each year. In the fall of 1990 Sue became chairman of the board, and her daughter, Claudia, and son, David, now share the copresidency.

Sue had been applying Attitudinal Healing principles in

her company long before she ever heard of the Center. Her maternal grandmother was by far her most important teacher and spiritual mentor. Sue was introduced to our center and some of our books by her daughter, Claudia, who volunteers her services with us. Sue began attending some of our meetings, went to one of our workshops, became a facilitator, and is now vice president of our board of directors.

When you first meet Sue, you know you are talking to a very remarkable woman, with a mind that works with lightning speed and whose inner light is crystal clear and visible to all.

In interviewing Sue in her home, we noticed that her face appeared bittersweet. On one hand you could see her exciting, wonderful sparkling eyes and most infectious smile, together with a sensitive, compassionate, tender face. On the other hand, her face revealed, in a very subtle way, that this was a person who had gone through great sorrow and grief.

And as she talked, there was a simple, clear, and direct honesty that radiated its authenticity through Sue's directness and lack of ambiguity when she spoke about what she thought and how she felt. It was like a breath of fresh air to feel the fullness and openness of her heart. She was not afraid to be vulnerable or to let others touch the very center of her heart.

Before sharing how she brings unconditional love and how she activates Attitudinal Healing principles in her company, we thought it would be helpful to mention something of Sue's past.

Sue was born in a very small town in Germany, called Landau, not very far from the French border. She was the youngest of three children, having an older sister and an older brother. Although her father could be very demanding and exacting, she was his favorite and she had a very close relationship with him. Her father expected a lot of himself as well as others, and Sue felt empowered by him. It was a very loving environment, but the biggest influence was the spiritual force of her grandmother.

Sue loved to visit her grandmother, and her grandmother often made the half-hour train trip to visit Sue. Sue said, "My grandmother was the most powerful example of unconditional love I have met. She just never made any judgments against anyone. She was 'absolute goodness,' and I never witnessed her taking sides when there was a disagreement or argument. It was the presence of peace in her that I admired the most.

"My grandmother had a very close connection to God. She really didn't talk about it that much or try to influence others in regard to God. She demonstrated her belief by her total acceptance of everyone.

"I remember with fondness her baking cookies and other goodies. It was such a good feeling to be around her, and when she hugged you, it felt like she took all of you in. She really listened, and I always knew that she would love and accept me totally no matter what I had done."

When Sue was eleven, two major things happened. First, her sister died of meningitis, and second, her brother, who was six years older than she, left home to attend school, leaving Sue an only child. Her parents spent a long time in grief but did not talk about it. One of the unspoken rules of the family was that you didn't share your feelings with anyone.

Sue told us, "I felt a lot about the things I couldn't talk about." Sue felt that her role in the family was to make everyone else feel happy by denying and suppressing her own feelings. Even when she was feeling tumultuous inside, she tried to wear a smile on her face because she believed it was her role to make others happy.

At about this same period of time Hitler came to power and began building his empire. As anti-Semitism spread like wildfire through the country, Sue found herself being ostracized even by her own best friends. As the situation became more difficult, an uncle from Buffalo, New York, arranged for Sue to travel to Holland and then to the United States.

Although her father knew that things were getting worse in his country, he did not choose to leave and later died in Germany from complications following surgery. Soon afterward Sue's mother joined her daughter in Buffalo. Sue's grandmother escaped to Holland after Hitler overran the lowlands, but was later sent to a concentration camp where she died in a Nazi gas chamber.

When we asked Sue how she has dealt with the pain of the past, she replied, "I am still dealing with it. There is part of me that doesn't think you have to hang on to pain, that we can learn from the past and then let go of it, but in many ways I am still holding on to it. I still cannot comprehend the depth of the Nazi atrocities and how human beings can be so cruel to each other.

"I have not even talked to my children about some of my experiences until recently. I guess I was in denial, and was not yet ready to deal with all those feelings. But I want to grow more, so now I am doing my best to explore what is going on inside. I want to learn more about the forgiveness process and to find ways to let go of all fear and judgments and be more creatively helpful to others."

Early in her life Sue discovered that she had natural talent as a designer. She worked for others for a while, then started her own business. Along the way she got married. Her husband later developed multiple sclerosis and had a very drawn-out illness before he died. It was another very challenging time for Sue. She did her best to take care of him at home and to work in her office. At the same time she tried to be cheerful.

BUSINESS

Sue's business continues to grow each year. She has made every effort to make use of all the learning experiences that life has given her. Always foremost in her mind was how miraculously fortunate she was to get out of Germany when so many others her age were killed in concentration camps.

Perhaps because of this she feels more motivated than most to make a difference in the world, to make a contribution. From the very beginning she has tried to maintain a "family atmosphere" in her business that includes all of her employees. She stated, "I would never ask anyone to do anything that I would not do. I always felt that we should do unto others as we would have them do unto us.

"At work I relate to each employee as part of my family. I have always believed that it was important that people have time at work to talk about what might be bothering them in their lives.

"I am very tuned in to my co-workers, and if I sense that anyone is having a slight bit of discomfort, I like to know what is causing it and see if I can be helpful in some way. Just giving people time and simply listening to them does wonders for good morale.

"Our mission statement is that we want our products to be responsive to the environment, and we want to foster employees' personal growth and development. This is the heartbeat of our company. We don't think it is effective to make people feel guilty. As a matter of fact we think that guilt is counterproductive. We don't beat people up and we don't yell at them.

"Being in the garment industry for so many years and experiencing what it was like to be in a yelling environment, I know that this was something I would never want in my company."

We asked Sue about profit sharing in her company, and she replied, "Everyone who has been working for us for more than a year is part of our profit-sharing plan. In addition to that we have a bonus plan twice a year—once at Christmastime and another at the end of our fiscal year, in April. And for a company our size I think we have one of the best health and pension plans going."

We asked, "If you were going to address the graduating class of the Harvard Business School, what might you say?"

Sue thought for a moment, then said, "I would tell them to know their craft and how to communicate clearly and yet have an open heart. I would suggest that they not make money the only bottom line. The bottom line is much more than that. It is the satisfaction of creating something that is useful to other people. We have kept our prices reasonable, designed attractive clothes, and have done it in such a way that they don't wear out easily. I would also explain my belief that to have both inner and outer success, it is important to share your profits with others.

"I would tell them about the satisfaction of seeing a baby that you created grow, and I'd emphasize that true growth only takes place when honesty, conscientiousness, and integrity are on the top of the list in all communication."

In reviewing our interview with Sue Siegel, what was most striking for us was the feeling of the presence of Sue's grandmother. We sometimes forget, with all the trials and tribulations of our lives, that there is often one person who has made a difference to us, who continues to give us the strength to continue having hope in a world that often not only looks unfriendly but is truly life-threatening.

Sue told us, "There is not a day that goes by that I don't think of my grandmother. In my own way I do my best to emulate her. I could not have had a better model."

Although it is clear that Sue brings into the business environment a caring, heartfelt attitude, we didn't want to give the impression that everything is always sweetness and light. She is feminine and she is strong. Sue can also be tough-minded, but never at another person's expense, never in an attacking way. She is direct and honest. It might not be what the other person would want to hear, but you can bet your life that it would be an honest communication.

COMPETITION

In most companies competition is the name of the game, with the key goal being to win in the marketplace. Perhaps one of the problems some businesses have today is that they still think of competition in its most destructive form. This usually means seeing your competitor as your enemy and doing everything you can to win over his or her customers, no matter what the cost. It means doing everything you can to make certain that you win and the other guy loses. Attitudes that encourage people to see value in competency are often snuffed out by the drive to annihilate their competitor.

Competition is being replaced by other attitudes that also begin with the letter *c*, such as caring, cooperation, compassion, and creativity. There is a new focus on excellence in all one's endeavors, rather than concentrating wholly on competition and what you can do to knock the other person out of the running.

There seems to be a spiritual unfolding that is most difficult to put into words. We are beginning to see positive results as companies on the cutting edge differentiate themselves from companies where the bottom line is limited to money and where goals are limited to serving the most selfish of interests.

The "form" of the new business is not yet clear, but the "connective" tissue within this form is becoming increasingly clear. It is full of heart, made up of caring, concern, and a willingness to be as helpful to others as we would like others to be to us. It is a consciousness focused on giving rather than on getting and a self-realization that comes when we do everything we can to empower everyone to be the most she or he can be.

AN ATTITUDE OF EQUALITY

Of the many companies that are finding new, more caring ways of doing business, Levi Strauss & Co. is one of the most frequently mentioned. Bob Haas and Levi Strauss truly believe that the bottom line has to be more than just money. Levi Strauss, a family-run company, has pioneered a way of doing business that demonstrates that it really is possible to make money and at the same time create an empowering work environment, characterized by caring, personal recognition, honesty, and responsibility. The connective tissue of this company is love and a caring, heartfelt attitude toward employees, the product, and the customer that is filled with integrity and responsibility.

Here is a company where every effort is made to respect and empower every employee and where everyone is an equal teacher-student, student-teacher to each other. The emphasis is on the positive, and leadership potential is encouraged in everyone. There is much emphasis on open communication between employees, with managers and workers at every level of employment mingling and speaking with each other to share their thoughts and feelings freely.

It was a wonderful experience to be escorted into the unpretentious office of the president and chairman of the board of Levi Strauss & Co. Very evident was a round table with some drawings of Bob Haas's eleven-year-old daughter, Elise.

Bob, who likes employees to call him by his first name, was dressed informally in sweater, shirt, and slacks. He told us that he would not let anything interfere with being at home with his daughter on her birthday. This family orientation is something that is emphasized throughout the company. It seems to us that a company that is able to reveal its heart in this way is a company that people really value working for.

One of the most exciting things for us to discover during our tour was "The Aspirations Statement of Levi Strauss & Co." This was not just a list of idle statements stuck in people's desk drawers where they were easily forgotten. These statements were the heartbeat of the company.

It was clear that these aspirations provided the rudder for guiding the infrastructure of a very flexible and responsive company. These statements defined company values that encouraged a caring atmosphere of dignity, personal recognition, responsibility, honesty, and mutual respect. They helped to create a style of communication between all employees where it was safe to disagree and share honest feedback. The golden thread running through every statement is empowerment for every individual, with the company fully supporting people in their own personal growth.

We felt this statement to be so important that we decided to quote it in its entirety:

THE ASPIRATIONS STATEMENT
OF LEVI STRAUSS & CO.

We all want a company that our people are proud of and committed to, where all employees have an opportunity to contribute, learn, grow, and advance based on merit, not politics or background. We want our people to feel respected, treated fairly, listened to, and involved. Above all, we want satisfaction from accomplishments and friendships, balanced personal and professional lives, and to have fun in our endeavors.

When we describe the kind of Levi Strauss & Co. we want in the future, what we are talking about is building on the foundation we have inherited: affirming the best of our company's traditions, closing gaps that may exist between principles and practices, and updating some of our values to reflect contemporary circumstances.

WHAT TYPE OF LEADERSHIP IS NECESSARY TO MAKE OUR ASPIRATIONS A REALITY?

New Behavior: Leadership that exemplifies directness, openness to influence, commitment to the success of others, willingness to acknowledge our own contributions to problems, personal accountability, teamwork, and trust. Not only must we model these behaviors but we must coach others to adapt them.

Diversity: Leadership that values a diverse work force (age, sex, ethnic group, etc.) at all levels of the organization, diversity in experience, and diversity in perspectives. We have committed to taking full advantage of the rich backgrounds and abilities of all our people and to promoting a greater diversity in position of influence. Differing points of view will be sought: diversity will be valued and honesty rewarded, not suppressed.

Recognition: Leadership that provides greater recognition— both financial and psychic—for individuals and teams that contribute to our success. Recognition must be given to all who contribute: those who create and innovate and also those who continually support the day-to-day business requirements.

Ethical Management Practices: Leadership that epitomizes the stated standards of ethical behavior. We must provide clarity about our expectations and must force these standards through the corporation.

Communications: Leadership that is clear about company, unit, and individual goals and performance. People must know what is expected of them and receive timely, honest feedback on their performance and career aspirations.

Empowerment: Leadership that increases the authority and responsibility of those closest to our products and customs. By actively pushing responsibility, trust, and recognition into the organization, we can harness and release the capabilities of all our people.

Clearly Levi Strauss is a company on the leading edge, one that is willing to let go of the old paradigm in which managers used their authority to manipulate people through fear, with all of the emphasis on control and very little attention given to listening and empowerment.

Levi Strauss was founded in 1850, and since its founding the Haas family has been the guiding light, helping to create a corporate culture that is an inspiration. The company continues a tradition of commitment to social values and to the creation of a positive work environment. Its philanthropic commitments are diverse and manifold. Its response to its employees with AIDS, as well as organizations helping those with AIDS, for example, has been outstanding, setting a standard for the entire business community.

Bob Haas told us an interesting story about empowerment at their Blue Ridge, Georgia, plant. The workers at this plant were told that they would share fifty-fifty in the savings that resulted from any ideas they contributed. In response employees at every level began looking for ways to improve efficiency and productivity. Management listened, just as they had promised they would do. And now many important improvements have taken place, making the Blue Ridge plant one of their best. Bob's corporate vision is to move in the direction of creating team-oriented, multiskilled environments where the team will collectively take on many of the tasks that were once the sole responsibility of supervisors and trainers.

Going through the company, one immediately gets the feeling of a happy family, where each member is valued and where it is obvious that people are enjoying their work and their growth. There is a respect for the dignity and growth capacity of each person. There is trust because, as much as possible, information is made available to all concerned, and there are no secrets. The "Aspirations Statement" is becoming the heartbeat of the organization, with every attempt to live by it and make it alive at all levels.

Bob shied away from answering questions about his spiritual beliefs or any spiritual pathway he might be following. He did not want to be categorized in any way. He did say, however, that his best teachers in life, those who could be seen as having something to do with his learning to express his spiritual essence, were his daughter and his wife.

What came through in the interview with Bob Haas was that this is a man who *walks his talk*, who truly lives his beliefs to the best of his abilities. He has an extremely clear focus on the values of integrity, honesty, caring, listening, collaborating, cooperating, and joint decision making. Also what was clear was his ability to share what he didn't know, his willingness to be vulnerable, his caring, and his laser-clear vision of hope, even during troubling times. He goes by the belief that when there is mutual empowerment and caring, there are no limits to growth.

COMPARTMENTALIZATION

More and more people are realizing the importance of no longer living compartmentalized, fragmented lives, in which they are one person during their hours at work and an entirely different person at home. Likewise many businesses are realizing that everyone benefits when there is greater harmony between personal and business life.

Increasing numbers of people are choosing to focus their

attention on living lives that are whole, in which interest in others is as important as self-interest, and such principles can be applied equally in both their business and their personal lives.

To Give Is to Receive

Fred Matser is a wonderful example of a person who has been involved in his own personal transformation process for a number of years now. More recently he has made every effort to bring his spiritual principles into every part of his life, including his business. Caring relationships, where there is equality and mutual respect for everyone with whom he communicates—from the person in an entry-level job on up to the board of directors—are now the rule rather than the exception, and there is much less compartmentalization.

Fred is a dear friend of ours from Holland. He is one of the larger real estate developers in the Netherlands, where both he and his company have been going through an amazing transformation. Until only a few years ago the power of making deals and accumulating money were his prime goals, and he did very well at both.

As he began to work very hard on the unfinished business in his personal life, he discovered that he had been spiritually empty. Fred began to see his interconnection with everything in the universe. He began to listen to an inner voice and to do his best to make all his decisions based on his own inner guidance. More and more Fred began to trust in a Higher Power, and his focus changed from making money to giving money away to help others.

In Switzerland he headed programs for the Red Cross and Red Crescent Societies, contributing his personal time and financial support. These programs deal with the reduction of child mortality and morbidity related to diseases involving diarrhea. As he began to be more helpful to others and gave more money to worthy causes, he found that he was spending less time in his business. An interesting phenomenon began to occur. His company began to make more money, which meant that more money was available for his philanthropic efforts.

Fred's attitudes toward his relationships, in both his personal and his business life, began to change. He began to learn how he could be creatively detached from having to be in control, involving himself in battles where there was always a winner and a loser.

Recently Fred had an opportunity to sell a 50 percent interest in a shopping center at a very attractive price. His other partners blocked the sale. Previously, he told us, he would have gotten very angry and would have gone to battle in defense of his own cause. This time he simply detached himself from the results and kept his peace of mind.

A couple of weeks later his partners returned to say that they had decided to sell.

More money than ever before is coming to him as he has changed his approach and attitudes toward other people. More than ever before Fred is really concentrating on having the same interest in others as he has in himself.

Another example that Fred shared with us involved a business transaction he was in the middle of negotiating. In the past he would have been under a great deal of stress. This time, however, his guidance was clear. He knew what the final financial terms were that he would accept, yet he was very relaxed, completely trusting the outcome of the negotiation.

The person with whom he was negotiating seemed to become angry, telling Fred, "I can't negotiate with you because you won't resist and argue with me." Fred replied, "I have said how I feel and I don't choose to fight." Later the other man broke down in tears and said, "I am so used to fighting when I negotiate. It is amazing for me to learn that it is possible to negotiate without fighting and without fear, and I thank you for this experience." As Fred pointed out, this turned out to be a "win-win" situation, since they found a solution that worked for both of them.

Recently Fred has made the decision to use more of his money for philanthropic causes. He is in the process of arranging his affairs so that he can spend all of his time in this endeavor. He not only believes but knows that giving and receiving are the same.

In the booklet that describes Fred's three philanthropic organizations, he writes the following:

> The chaos in the environment is a reflection of the disorder in our heads and in our hearts. Over the past years I have come to realize more and more that everything is connected to everything and that the driving force behind everything is unconditional love. If man were to let go of fear, the beauty of the earth would manifest itself more fully again.

Fred added that in giving this advice he is also very aware that every day he still falls flat on his face. As people doing business are finding a willingness to do what they can to help bring about more joining and harmony, the experiences of teachers like Sue Siegel, Bob Haas, and Fred Matser are becoming increasingly important to us all. These people and thousands more like them are our guides, providing us with valuable markers that light the pathway ahead.

We asked Fred what advice he might give to a young person going into business today, and he responded with the following, which we think provides a wonderful set of affirmations:

Affirmations
1. Always share.
2. Always impart something of your own self into what you do . . . not just money.
3. Have joy in what you do.
4. Trust in your Higher Power and you will be provided with abundance.
5. Trust your instincts and make choices that you feel good about.

❖

CHANGING ATTITUDES IN BUSINESS—PART II

*Letting go of previous boundaries,
transforming competition into compassion
and cooperation, and supporting
the unlimited growth of the individual
may be some of the greatest challenges
that face the business world.*

New Attitudes in the Workplace

We would like to touch on just a few of the factors that seem to create problems in the workplace, in particular those elements that seem to cause a sense of separation and that may inhibit personal empowerment, value, and growth.

Although our society has benefited from tremendous technological and scientific advances during the twentieth century, many of which have allowed businesses to grow into global institutions, at times there have been significant things lacking in the core and the heartbeat of the business environment. This can best be described as a spiritual emptiness, resulting from a neglect of the *human* aspects of business.

It used to be that the name of the game in business was to win at any cost, and it made no difference who got hurt in the process. Today there is a new awakening, a belief that there has to be another way of looking at the world, another way of relating to each other, and another way of conducting business that is not limited by our own self-centered interests. This awakening is occurring because there is growing awareness that the old vertical, pyramid structure of operating a corporation—with a few people at the top who have all the power and a lot of people at the bottom with no power—simply doesn't work anymore.

There is a growing influx of new attitudes in the workplace. This includes a renewed interest in personal growth that benefits not just the company but the individual as well. There is a new awareness of the fact that personal empowerment, mutual respect, and more open communications are the source of strength for everyone across the board. These are attitudes that used to be limited to the top echelon, the chosen few in power at the top of the pyramid. Now there is more movement in companies to have an equal concern for all—workers, suppliers, and customers alike.

There Is No Value in Guilt or Blame

John Robinson, chairman of the board and past president of the San Francisco–based Harper Group, recently featured in *Forbes* magazine, has been a friend of mine (Jerry's) for many years. His wife, Patsy, helped start the Center for Attitudinal Healing back in 1975. John and I meet at 6:30 every Thursday morning that we are both in town and consult with each other. He has been a welcome supporter of our work and has endeavored to incorporate many of our Attitudinal Healing principles into his business.

John has put into operation, both in his business and in his personal life, a willingness to believe that our minds hold no limitations, that our thoughts create our own reality, and that we are responsible for what we experience. He has demonstrated the value of recognizing that we limit ourselves when we hold on to grievances and unforgiving thoughts and that we empower ourselves when we forgive. John believes that nothing is impossible and that our thoughts create our reality.

John writes a monthly letter to his more than 3,500 employees telling them not only what is happening within the company but also about his family. John has also created a beautiful facility called Retreat Place, just north of Russian River in northern California, where in-service trainings go on throughout the year. Many of his staff are sent out to colleges, universities, and training centers for further education. John believes in doing his part to provide his employees with opportunities for enriching their lives.

John has created a health letter for his company that has encouraged his employees all around the world to take more responsibility for their health, resulting in fewer hours lost due to illness. In the letter people are told about ways to improve their health through diet and exercise and are given ways to change their attitudes and style of living.

John truly believes in letting go of all negative thoughts and creating positive mental pictures—visions that are filled with possibility rather than limitation or doubt. His company has become extremely successful and continues to grow.

REMOVING GUILT

It used to be that everyone in John's company hated going to budget meetings, afraid that their head would get chopped off by John. After a conversation we had one day about the negative effects of motivating people through fear and guilt, John changed his attitude and announced that no longer were there going to be guilt trips placed on others. Instead people would be encouraged to take a very different approach and to look upon mistakes and errors as ways for everyone to learn. To encourage this new approach, he even went so far as to share some of his own mistakes with others.

There was an immediate shift in everyone's attitudes. Employees were no longer afraid to come to budget meetings. Everyone began to learn that you can't grow without making mistakes, and that mistakes are simply errors to be corrected, not something to feel guilty about or to try to cover up by finding someone else to blame. Mistakes were then more easily corrected. In an environment where people were able to bring their mistakes out into the open, rather than hiding them, everyone could learn from the errors. More progress than ever was made.

THE VALUE OF DEFENSELESSNESS

One morning I saw John just before he was going to a stockholders' meeting. He had heard that they were upset about some information they believed had been withheld from them, and he had been meeting with his lawyers to determine what defensive strategies he might take.

I suggested to John that there were alternatives to seeing the stockholders as his enemy. He could choose to see them as fearful and wanting to be better informed. I shared an affirmation stating, "In my defenselessness my safety lies." The other option I suggested was not to be defensive but to share the truth. He called me later that day to say that the meeting turned out to be a tranquil, peaceful, successful, and productive one. John learned his lesson well and continues to tell others about the importance of defenselessness.

John has also learned the value of being still an instant and going inside ourselves to listen to our inner voice, our intuitive selves, when making decisions. John Robinson makes most of his major decisions based on the gut feeling he gets this way.

There is not one of us who does not get caught up in our outside worlds and with the business of the day. It seems almost impossible to stop and be still, to make decisions based on our inner guidance. John makes it a point not to get caught up in yesterday's bad news. Instead he believes in creating his own history in the present moment, thus freeing himself of the feeling that he has to act like a robot whose actions are limited by a computer program based on what happened yesterday or even in years past.

John knows that a disciplined mind is a free and balanced mind. He disciplined himself to exercise and run every day, and he watches his food intake, eating only healthy foods. He looks much younger than his chronological age because he believes you are as young as you believe your heart is. Every day is a brand-new, wonderful, and challenging day for John. He is not a person who would know the meaning of the word *boredom*.

John believes that for companies to be successful, they must become more aware of their global citizenship and have a caring attitude, not only within one's own company and community but for the entire world. John maintains that successful companies are those that truly. concentrate on service and meeting the needs of others.

It can be helpful to keep in our minds, at all times, the belief that we are all teachers to each other. Businesses can be especially good teachers because each one of them is like a community in itself. It is a like a laboratory of people living and working together, a place where the beliefs we hold in our minds really can make a difference in all of our lives, regardless of which side of the counter we find ourselves.

MELBA BEALS

Melba Beals has been in public relations for over fifteen years, and the lesson she offers is that it is possible to bring one's most strongly felt spiritual beliefs into the business arena—even in an area as competitive as advertising—and be successful at the same time. Melba's story is inspiring, not only because she has been very successful in business but also because she is a writer with a real contribution to make to society. As a teenager growing up in Little Rock, Arkansas, she was one of nine black children escorted by the military to school during the 1957 Civil Rights advances. Melba feels that, frightening though that experience was, it has made her strong.

When we interviewed Melba, she stated, "I think that all of my life I have been on a spiritual pathway. At first I had some difficulty integrating my personal spiritual pathway with my business. So when I started my business, I was coming from 'scarcity' and I would say yes to almost anyone who wanted my services, if their requests were not illegal or immoral. I began to make a good living, but one day I thought to myself that I really wasn't doing anything to make this world a better place in which to live. I then decided with every part of me that I was going to do something about that.

"I discovered that I couldn't feel peaceful inside if I did not live in integrity in both my personal and my business life. It was then that I started to interview my potential clients to determine if I wanted to work for them. Public relations firms put words out into the universe. That is their job. I decided that I did not want to do this unless the words served humanity.

"I never worked for companies that sold tobacco and alcohol. I stopped working for individuals or companies whose intent was not to contribute positively to the universe. I made up my mind that I was going to serve God by serving others. I would not put any more trash out into the media. "When I interview my clients, I ask them how their product serves others. I ask them, 'Is this a product that you would want your mother to buy?' I try to determine if there is integrity in the company and in the products.

"I now feel there is a congruity between my personal and my business life. I feel happier and more peaceful about life. I see relationships now as teachers sent to me for my further learning. And I am learning all the time. I do not see how the world can operate without forgiveness. It has to be an integral part of our business and personal lives. I am committed to living that edict."

We have known Melba for many years. She has many times offered her services free for our project, Children as Teachers of Peace. Melba is a beautiful light who brings her spirituality with her wherever she goes. Her last statement to us was, "Some people told me that I was too kind to make it in the world of business. I believe I have proved them wrong. I think that kindness is your strength, not your weakness."

THE NEW HUMANIZATION OF WORK RELATIONSHIPS

In the past and even today there has been an unspoken rule in business that states, "Never show your true feelings." There is a very old slogan, one that still goes around, that says, "If you want to get to the top, learn to have a thick skin."

Another unwritten law that has trapped many people, particularly if they happened to be at the top, was, "Always act as if you are perfect but everyone else is a screwup." The idea was to associate only with people on a horizontal axis, that is, with people who were at least your "equals" in terms of money, influence, and social status. You were to shy away from associations with anyone beneath your level in the corporate structure. These attitudes produced highly manipulative relationships, where people were treated as objects.

CONNIE BOUCHER

Connie Boucher is one of the most inspiring, delightful, and determined people you would ever want to meet. She started her company in 1960 with no money and a lot of determination. Knowing Connie, it comes as no surprise that she found a name for her firm that reflects something about her innermost beliefs: Determined Productions. It is an important lesson in the power of the attitude of determination that she offers us in her story.

The company has grown steadily over the last three decades, expanding from three employees to three hundred. It's a family business. Connie chairs the board, and her son, Douglas, is president. Determined designs, manufactures, and licenses a wide assortment of toys, books, dolls, apparel, and other accessories for children and adults. It is perhaps best known for its products featuring the "Peanuts" comic strip cast and its merchandise inspired by writer-illustrator Joan Walsh Anglund.

When asked what problems she has encountered as a woman in the business world, Connie replied, "Sometimes I think it is helpful to be a little naive. You see, I didn't know there might be problems for a woman in business when I launched Determined Productions. I just knew in my heart that I had energy, determination, and the vision to make a company work. I never let other people steer me away from my goal. I've never thought that anything was impossible. I don't believe there is anything a person can't do."

We are convinced that anyone who has spent time with Connie would immediately feel her unstoppable energy and her zest for life. She has an attitude of total belief in herself, and she leaves no room for self-doubt.

BELIEVING IN OURSELVES

We asked Connie where she thought she might have gotten her drive and self-confidence. She immediately began to talk about her mother. "I received much encouragement from both my parents, but it was my mom who really inspired me. My mother was a college graduate and a Phi Beta Kappa. She was always totally involved in one project or another. Years ago she wrote for *Sunset* magazine and became very active in the Girl Scouts.

"My mom continued to work as director of Determined's Direct Mail Division until two weeks before her death. She was eighty-seven when she died."

We asked Connie to tell us about her philosophy for directing the company. She thought for a moment, then said, "What is most important is your relationship with people. I think it's possible to run a company where people truly care about one another. I try to treat everyone in my company like family."

We talked about the ratio of women and men in her company. Connie told us it was divided evenly, with perhaps one or two more women than men. She went on to say that she had stipulated to her company in Japan that more women must be hired for key executive positions.

AN ATTITUDE OF CARING

We asked Connie if she felt that she brought spiritual principles into the workplace, and if she did, what were her beliefs in this area. She replied, "My grandfather was a liberal minister of the Swedish Mission church. He felt very strongly that you give what you receive, that you treat others as you would have them treat you. Although I'm not a churchgoing person, I believe that there is something that is bigger than all of us that we just don't fully understand.

"I try to bring these principles into our business. For example, I feel I must give back something in return for all the wonderful things that have happened to me during my business life. So, Determined has become very involved with a variety of cause-related organizations, including UNICEF and the World Wildlife Fund. We have created product lines for both UNICEF and WWF. A portion of each sale goes directly to the organization. I try to show my appreciation to my employees by providing good benefits. I think our health benefits and profit-sharing plan are among the best.

"I think that relationships are of prime importance. However, I must admit that sometimes there are still those days when I have trouble practicing forgiveness. I think forgiveness plays an important role—both in business and in our personal lives."

We asked, "After you are gone, what would you like people to remember about you?"

She replied, "That I cared about others."

ADVICE TO OTHERS

We asked what advice she might offer young people who are thinking about going into the field of business. Connie replied, "I would tell them to put all of their heart into what they're doing and to work hard. Don't let other people talk you out of your dream.

"Above all else, believe in yourself and know that nothing is impossible and that there are no limits. Be enthusiastic. Never give up hope. Be concerned with what is happening to the planet and to people who may be less fortunate than you, and be willing to do something about it. Make kind, gentle, nourishing relationships your goal and recognize the importance of forgiveness."

The last question we asked was, "Of all the many things you have done, what makes you feel the most proud?" Connie paused for a moment before she replied, "I haven't thought about that before, but I think that what makes me feel most proud is that I have developed a very successful business and I have become a role model for other women. It is so important for women not to give up their power.

"The second thing that occurs to me is that I am proud

of my children and my grandchildren. My five grandchildren go everywhere with me. Of course, everything's not perfect, but we're a very close family, and I'm happy about that."

There is no question in our minds that Connie's success and the success of her multimillion-dollar company, Determined Productions Inc., has much to do with key attitudes that she holds in her heart and mind. These are: (a) Let go of negative thoughts from the past; (b) believe in yourself and never think that nothing is impossible; and (c) believe that the reason we are here is to care for and help others. Connie continues to be a wonderful teacher to all who know her.

RELATIONSHIP PROBLEMS IN BUSINESS

Of all the many problems in the business world today, most authorities agree that at or near the top of the list is *relationships*. Relationships at work not only affect productivity, they also can make the difference between having a mind that is always in turmoil, unable to focus on the present, and having a mind that is at peace. There are many relationship problems in our homes that get displaced into our business life and vice versa. So, while we may not immediately think of our relationships as business issues, many business experts suggest that how we relate to others needs to be given top priority.

There is ample evidence that our attitudes about others are but a reflection of our attitudes about ourselves. There are many of us who have been divorced for whom the relationship remains unhealed. Our unhealed emotions can be easily displaced to our business lives, where it's easy to find a dumping ground for the bitterness and resentment that we still hold in our hearts.

There are still many unhealed relationships in which we abused others or in which others may have abused us. There are those who have attempted to climb the ladder of success by walking over other people. Or perhaps we are holding bitterness in our hearts because others have walked over us. Regardless of who has done the walking, and who has been walked over, those relationships may still remain unhealed.

There are many of us who have gained great success in the external world yet our inner success has escaped us and our personal lives remain in a shambles. There are many who are running through life, always in such a rush that we are rarely at peace. And there are those of us who appear to have successful and satisfying business and personal lives, who seem to have many friends, but still have no one with whom to really share their most intimate thoughts and feelings. And they continue to go on living lonely, fragmented, and separated lives.

As You Help Others, You Heal Yourself

Don Carlson of Orinda, California, has long been known for his commitment to making this world a better place in which to live, and his story continues to convince everyone who hears it that this ideal can be a realistic one in business. For many years he was chief executive officer and chairman of the board of Consolidated Capitals. Don told us during our interview with him that the bottom line of his company was always much deeper than money and that he had striven to make relationships and service to others one of the top priorities of his company.

Don stated that everything was done to create the best work environment possible. The company had such things as a gymnasium, basketball courts, racquetball court, and many other apparatuses where employees could work out, keeping their bodies and minds healthy and alert during the working hours. In addition, the company would pay for any college course that any employee wanted to take, and it did not have to be business-oriented.

The company did much to recognize employees for their contributions at all levels. They offered everyone opportunities to buy stock in the company, and they empowered individuals to make decisions. The company was like a car-

ing family where there was great respect for the creativeness
and usefulness of all employees. Every effort was made not
to make others guilty when mistakes occurred, and everyone
was encouraged to learn from his or her mistakes.

Don Carlson has been on a spiritual quest for many years.
He does not belong to any religious organization, and it
would be a mistake to attempt to categorize him. There is,
however, no question in our minds that his journey for
spiritual fulfillment has played a subtle yet definite role in
the management of the company with which he has been
affiliated for so many years. Don mentioned that forgiveness
has a definite place in the workplace as well as in one's
personal life.

Don and his company are concerned about the planet
and about giving to others. Over the years they have been
involved in many community activities, including tutoring
programs and Special Olympics. As far as Don's spiritual
journey is concerned, he said, "We are all spiritual creatures
caught up in this bag of bones and skin. I believe that our
journey here is to be as helpful as we can to others, and
while I chose business as my vehicle, I tried to be a good
friend to a lot of people and to do things in my life that
were as helpful as they could be, to as many people as
possible."

Don has created a nonprofit organization called ARKS,
which contributes to worthy causes where people are doing
their best to make a difference in the world, bringing love
and a caring attitude to others in need. Don does his best
to put his spiritual beliefs into action, continuing to be helpful to many different organizations that are devoted to service for others.

The last question we asked Don was, "What advice
would you give a graduating class in a business college?"
He replied, "I would tell them to trust in themselves, and
I would remind them that we are all spiritual beings and
we are all part of God. And if we trust that fact and allow
our feeling to be the barometer of our thoughts and actions,
we will always come up with the right answers in the long
run."

BE A LOVE FINDER RATHER THAN A FAULT FINDER

Warren Wertheimer demonstrates that it really is possible to be a love finder rather than a fault finder in the world of business as well as in our personal relationships. He is owner of the Rolling Hills Club, a family, multisport club in Novato, California. I (Jerry) have known Warren for many years and have been a witness to his spiritual transformation, which has also transformed his business.

In the eyes of most people who knew him before his transformation, Warren was a rather powerful man, who could be provocative and demanding. He could easily become angry and lose his temper, and it often appeared that he only cared about himself. He seemed to have a need to live the kind of life where he was always controlling other people.

He became a student of *A Course in Miracles* and began to use it as his tool for spiritual transformation. He attended group meetings on the Course that were, at one time, held at our center. One night he talked about his anger and distress concerning his son's behavior. His son was acting out, and his behavior took the form of stealing.

Warren remembered my telling him to consider the possibility of going inside himself and asking for help by asking, What would it take to create a loving environment for both me and my son? He did this and he later told me that the answer he received was, Do the things that will allow you to feel loving toward your son.

In essence Warren began that day to be a love finder rather than a fault finder. And it worked. The relationship between him and his son began to improve tremendously. His son's self-esteem climbed, his grades improved, and he became a successful computer programmer. Warren stated that as his son's and his relationship improved, he began to learn much about the value of forgiving others and himself.

Warren later found that he could begin to apply these same spiritual principles in a very practical way in the day-to-day business of running his tennis club. These new awarenesses became integrated into the operating principles of the club. Both Warren and his employees agreed to take responsibility for creating a loving environment and to recognize that there were always choices of seeing a disturbing situation differently.

For example, when a club member calls up and is angry, appearing to attack, Warren or his staff attempts to see that person as fearful and giving a call of help for love. When both employees and members stopped seeing events as personal attacks and that it was safe to be defenseless, most problems began to be solved effortlessly.

Members and employees are encouraged to be honest with their feelings with each other and not to have "withholds." They are encouraged to attempt to go in the direction of finding a loving space for the other person within their hearts. The prevailing attitude is to concentrate on positive thoughts rather than negative ones and that people are responsible for their own feelings.

Warren is interested in creating opportunities where everyone can grow. He has outside speakers come in to talk and dialogue on a host of different subjects. Warren also believes that giving is receiving and has been most kind in offering his club "free" for the Center's Christmas parties. Warren has found that the same spiritual principles can work very effectively in both his personal and his business life.

More and more companies, large and small, are demonstrating the new consciousness in the business community. They are taking an active role in demonstrating helpful and caring attitudes toward the community and the world in which they live. Appearing on the horizon are companies like Patagonia Sportswear, Ben and Jerry's Ice Cream, and the Body Shop, who devote appreciable money to save the environment and to help Third World countries.

People everywhere are finding that solutions to their own problems often come when they recognize that giving, caring, loving, and a willingness to help others take out the bumps and pave the road for a much easier journey. It is a journey where we learn one of the most fundamental truths of all—that to give is to receive.

THE NEW PARADIGM IN BUSINESS—
GUIDELINES FOR ALL OF US

There was a wonderful book that came out in 1990. The title is *Creative Work: The Constructive Role of Business in Transforming Society*. It was written by an old friend of ours, futurist Willis Harman, and his coauthor John Hormann. The book includes observations by Stan Janger and Amy Edmondson and is one of the best books we have seen about spiritual transformation in business. We were able to interview Willis, John, and Stan for this book.

Willis Harman has been instrumental in forming the World Business Academy, which allows business people who are on the cutting edge of the new business paradigm to share their viewpoints and learn from each other. One of the problems that we have to deal with is that the real value of what we do frequently does not show up in ways that can be measured and counted.

We asked Stan Janger if he would share with us some of his observations about companies that were involved in their own transformation—which meant taking a healthy look at all their old values and attitudes with a willingness to make a shift. He stated that they were usually organizations where the employees, the management, and the owners felt empowered and enjoyed their work and experiencing the fruits of their labors.

Willis, John, and Stan stated that the old Western industrial paradigm has begun to crumble because of the following:

- It failed to meet the basic condition that every citizen have the opportunity to be a full and valued participant, with the feeling of belonging and being useful.
- It failed to achieve, over the long term, a satisfactorily equitable distribution of power and wealth.
- It failed to give the contemporary person the sense of being a useful and necessary member of a social whole that in turn is geared into a meaningful plan

of existence within the totality of a cosmic or divine order.

Some of the suggested solutions that came from their book were:

- The promotion of integrity, creativity, trust, and co-operation—beyond vicious competition, pressure, manipulation, and deceit.

- A reduction in the bureaucracy within large organizations—beyond the concept of "Trust is good; control is better."

- The promotion of values and incentives that foster care of the earth: its life-support processes, its resources, its wilderness, and its beauty—beyond the concept of the earth as subject to human desires.

- If the fundamental fact about us is that we are spiritual beings in a spiritual universe and the modern denial of this is in fact in error, then any social structure that is built around that denial will in the end fail to be satisfactory.

CHANGING ATTITUDES

There is a temptation to lose our peace of mind, not just in business but in every aspect of our lives. Most of us need all the help we can get to remind us that the attitudes we have are our own choices.

We have compiled the following list of negative attitudes that can inhibit peace of mind and create separation.

Attitudes That Create Separation

We create separation in our lives anytime:

- We believe that yelling and attacking others gets us what we want.

- We believe that our own interests should come before those of others.
- We choose to be unforgiving about another person's behavior or we are unforgiving about ourselves.
- We hide information from each other about what is going on in the company or participate in spreading rumors.
- Employees are not allowed to participate in the profitability of the company.
- We treat other people as objects or we are not treated as useful and creative.
- We do not believe in ourselves; and whenever we lack faith and trust.
- Only the top echelon is allowed to participate in decision making.
- We believe that manipulating others is a satisfactory way to communicate.
- We judge others throughout the day—even by holding judgmental thoughts about them in our minds.

The following list is to remind us of the ways we can create joining and peace of mind in every area of our lives.

Attitudes for Enhancing Peace, Growth, and Joining

We can enhance peace and joining:

- As employees—by having an attitude in which there is a level of creativity and responsibility as if we owned the company ourselves
- As an employer—by having an attitude of wanting to create the kind of company where we would like to be employees
- By being responsible for our own success and committed to the success of others
- By being willing to see others as loving or fearful and giving a call for help

- By living each day with honesty, integrity, and having a sense of harmony in what we think, say, and do
- By being willing to forgive ourselves and others; and being willing to let go of the shadows of the past, seeing others and ourselves only in the present
- Through our willingness to listen to others without judgment
- Through our willingness to be loving and caring of others and ourselves
- Through our willingness not to categorize people in negative ways
- Through our willingness to live one day at a time, neither judging others nor condemning ourselves

❖

CHAPTER THIRTEEN

Aging—Keeping the Child's Heart Alive Within Us

*In the long run we shape our lives
and we shape ourselves. The process never ends
until we die. And the choices we make
are ultimately our own responsibility.*

—Eleanor Roosevelt

FEAR OF AGING

We live in a youth-oriented culture, and the emphasis on eternal youthfulness has generated a fear of the aging process that is perhaps unprecedented in history. Advertisements on television, in magazines, and in the newspapers encourage us to do everything we can to prevent the appearance of growing old. We are encouraged to attack wrinkles and sagging flesh with plastic surgery. In fact, plastic surgery to forestall the appearance of aging is available for nearly every part of the body.

Many of us who have elderly parents, or who have a spouse or other loved one with one of the illnesses, such as Alzheimer's, that are associated with aging, may become very fearful. Not only are we deeply concerned about the course of their lives, but secretly we think of the possibility that "someday this could happen to me." Certainly one of the biggest fears that many of us have about growing old is losing control of our mental and physical faculties.

The fear of being useless is also a big issue as we enter our senior years. Employment practices in business and industry tend to create the impression among so many of us that the usefulness of our lives ends at a certain age. For example, in the airline industry, pilots are forced to retire at age sixty. Many other businesses force their employees to retire at sixty-five.

Since much of our self-esteem is involved with what we do in the world, forced retirement can cause us to feel that our lives are over. We don't necessarily send ourselves this message in a conscious way, but we may suddenly feel decreased energy and depression. Just the thought of being forced to retire at a particular age can put us into the position of suddenly not feeling useful or valuable anymore. Many people facing their retirement years describe the feeling as "being put out to pasture to finish our days quietly out of the way of the rest of the world."

Although the problems of decreased energy and depression may at first look like organic problems, treatable only by medication, they often turn out to be attitudinal in nature. Put another way, the feelings often associated with the aging process often have more to do with attitudes around self-esteem than they do with what actually happens to us physically and mentally as we grow older. When we see how true this is, we also see that there really is another way of looking at the aging process and that it is possible to heal those attitudes that limit us in the second half of our lives.

PERSONAL REFLECTIONS

My (Jerry's) interest in aging came from the fact that my father lived ninety-two years, and my mother was just shy of ninety-eight when she died, just a few years ago. Prior to their deaths both my parents lost their sight.

Both my parents taught me a lot about the challenges of aging. Some of the lessons I learned were among the hardest, yet most valuable ones in my life.

My own script for my parents was that their last years should be pleasant ones, with no health problems. After they had worked so hard and unselfishly for their children for so many years, I believed that they should be able to be happy and enjoy their old age. My script did not work out because both of my parents had many health problems and they perceived aging as their enemy, not their friend. I finally had to let go of my own script for them and discover a deeper meaning of the word *acceptance*.

There were many painful decisions that my brothers and I had to make in my parents' behalf. My dad spent his last years with my brother Art and his wife, Peggy, and my mom spent her last years in a home for senior citizens in San Francisco. There were always tremendous temptations for me to feel guilty about any decisions my brothers and I made about our parents.

As our population continues to live longer, thousands and thousands of families are challenged to face problems similar to those we faced. We are all having to take another, closer look at our own attitudes about aging.

There are those of us who may not have to make these difficult decisions right now. But as we think about the future, we may already feel some of the pain and confusion around the myriad issues that might arise, not only where our parents and spouses are concerned but where our own aging is involved.

PATIENCE, TENDERNESS, GENTLENESS, AND ACCEPTANCE

We will not find ourselves patient, tender, gentle, and accepting if we are still holding on to grievance, anger, and resentment, no matter how hard we may try to disguise it. It is indeed very difficult to be loving and helpful to our parents when we still have unfinished business with them from our childhoods. If our parents are elderly and sickly, we may try to be helpful and loving, but if we are still blaming our parents in any way, we will probably end up in conflict, which gets expressed in either external or internal battles. Help that comes only from feelings of duty and obligation does not necessarily bring love.

If for any reason our parents can push buttons in us that lead to conflict and despair, it is important to realize that we are the ones that made the button. There are many of us who still wish that our parents had been different—less critical, less rejecting, and more loving. There are those who have suffered from physical brutality, incest, and emotional and spiritual abuse. It is most important not to deny our feelings but rather to honor our rage and resentment. Eventually, if we wish to apply Attitudinal Healing principles in our lives, we are going to have to ask ourselves the question Does what seems to me to be justified anger and rage bring me peace of mind? If the answer is no, we may want to find ways to forgive the past and any dark shadows we may find in others or ourselves.

Today there are many support groups, at our centers as well as elsewhere, that help people work through difficult feelings about the past. Forgiveness that might once have seemed completely impossible not infrequently becomes a reality. Often there is a recognition that if we had gone through the same parenting and environment that our parents had experienced when they were kids, we might have made the same mistakes that they did. Perhaps we all try to do the best job we can as parents, based on the circumstances from which we came.

There are many elderly parents who continue to be critical of their grown children, seemingly trying to make them feel guilty every step of the way. There are many times that we, as adult children, still have that little kid inside of us that continues to seek our parents' approval and acceptance. We may even find ourselves feeling angry when we don't get the respect and love we want from our parents.

Our perceptions of ourselves and our parents begin to change when we can perceive them as fearful rather than angry, attacking, and disagreeable.

When we can choose not to see ourselves as victims, and can choose instead to see our parents as very powerful teachers of patience and acceptance, we can begin to experience peace of mind. This means accepting our parents' choice to be complaining, miserable, and blaming. When we know in our hearts, without the shadow of a doubt, that the essence of our being is love, we then know that we cannot be hurt. Rather than seeing the external mask and costume that our parents are putting out to us, we can choose to see their true essence of love.

Love is always tender, gentle, and patient. And the essence of this love is that we no longer feel any need of control issues. We are then free to be uplifted by finding acceptance in our heart, acceptance that is translated into the action of unconditional love.

There is a wonderful saying that comes from the Eastern spiritual teachings: "Don't push the river." When we flow with the river and stop trying to push upstream against the current, we begin to be gently surrounded by peace. That gentle reminder has been helpful to us in letting go of control issues with ourselves and our parents.

I (Jerry) found peace with my mom when I stopped trying to change her and stopped thinking that the only way I could have inner peace was if she changed.

At the time of this writing my (Diane's) mother and stepfather are in their seventies. They are both in excellent health and are fully involved in life. There have been many times, however, when I became preoccupied with the future and wondered how they would handle it if they developed serious health problems or a lingering terminal illness. I also wondered what my reactions would be and hoped that I would be able to be helpful in an empowering way.

What was very clear to me after I really looked at it was that I was full of fear about what would or wouldn't occur in the future. My mind would often play out a score of scenarios, some of them very depressing. I felt very helpless for a number of years because I didn't feel I could do anything to prevent my worst fears from coming true. All the possibilities I imagined seemed completely beyond my control.

It brought on a feeling of helplessness because I not only couldn't control their actual aging process, but, what was worse, I couldn't control my own. It wasn't until I realized that it was my *attitudes about aging* that were depressing me that I finally did something about it. Even if I couldn't control what was going on outside me, I certainly could do something to be more peaceful about what was happening inside.

I began to become involved with my parents in planning their years up to the time of their passing, which in turn gave me the insight and courage to plan my own final years. Today these concerns are no longer an issue, and I am confident that each day I will have the guidance and the tools necessary for accomplishing whatever challenges arise.

FEAR OF BEING ABANDONED

The fears of being separated, of feeling alone and abandoned, are common for many older people who are dependent on others to care for their basic needs. People who work in nursing homes, who provide care for older people, say that one of the biggest problems for their residents is that their family and loved ones visit only infrequently, or in many cases not at all.

Some people avoid visiting their parents because it is often a painful experience. They find it difficult to see not only their own parents but all the others who are sitting in chairs, staring into space, obviously feeling isolated, depressed, and perhaps confused. Anyone with a parent in a nursing home will usually admit that he doesn't want to visit because of his own feelings of helplessness and even guilt. We also don't want to be reminded of our own fears of what might happen to us as we grow older.

So often older people in nursing homes never get hugged or even touched. On a recent visit to a home we met a man in his nineties staring at a parrot in a cage. To us the man and the parrot both looked very sad. Our perceptions were that the man might very well have been identifying with the bird in the cage. Both of them felt trapped and limited.

How we treat the elderly is a direct reflection of our youth orientation, which includes our denial of the fact that we are all getting older. Few could disagree with the fact that our attitudes about aging need a comprehensive overhaul.

Mary Cole

At the time when I (Jerry) was having some frustrating times trying to create a happier environment for my parents, I received a visit from a wonderful woman who was eighty-two years old. She had recently moved from Los Angeles to a retirement home in Mill Valley. Her name was Mary Cole, and she was vibrant, enthusiastic, and full of zest. I remember that her energy seemed more like that of a spunky teenager than of a person in her eighties.

Mary told me that after reading two of my books, *Love Is Letting Go of Fear* and *Teach Only Love*, she felt a strong inner guidance to move up to northern California so that she could be near our Center for Attitudinal Healing. She said that she wanted our help starting an Attitudinal Healing group in a retirement home she had chosen to live in, called the Redwoods.

Mary observed that many people in retirement homes felt like they were victims. They felt that they had been discarded by their children, dumped in a place where they did not want to live. Mary said that most people in this situation end up being preoccupied with their physical ailments, always complaining about some bodily part. She thought that they were fearful of dying but afraid to talk about it.

Mary said that so many of her friends in the nursing home seemed to be living in the hurtful past. They had become bitter, angry, and resentful about life, and they felt abandoned not only by their families but by God as well.

Mary told us, "I really like your Attitudinal Healing principles, and I try to practice them each day of my life. And you know what, they really work! I particularly like the concept of 'This instant is the only time that there is' and 'As you learn to help others, you learn to help yourself.'

"I just know in my heart that if these people would just get out of their preoccupation with their bodies and start to help each other, they would begin to feel better about themselves, their lives, and each other."

She went on to say, "You see, I don't think that the problems with aging have so much to do with the body as they do with our state of mind and the attitudes we hold in it. I just know if these people stop blaming God and their children for their unhappiness and take responsibility for themselves, they will stop having all those 'pity parties.'

"As for me, I don't think much about my chronological age. What I think is important is keeping your heart full of love and being grateful for all the blessings and challenges that life presents to us.

"I think we need to teach each other that how we feel has little to do with the aging of our bodies. In fact it has a great deal to do with how much love we have in our hearts, how willing we are to be grateful for life and the challenges it presents us, and how willing we are to give our love and a helping hand to others."

As Mary talked, I smiled to myself because I thought of how well she put the principles of Attitudinal Healing into simple, practical use in her daily life. Mary also told me of her great faith in God. She said, "When you are helping and loving others, no matter how big or little the things you are doing, it's God's work. Then there is so much joy that any complaint you might have simply disappears."

Mary reminded us of a statement that Mother Teresa once shared with us: "We can do no great things, only small things with great love."

Mary Cole was like a breath of fresh air to me, and I was more than eager to join her in her efforts. This was back in 1979, and the groups are still going strong at the Redwoods. Mary died about five years ago, but her presence is always with us.

Some years ago Hugh Downs had a program on Public Television that focused on older citizens and what they were doing to help themselves. Before Mary died, we were privileged to be on that program with her and other members of the group she had helped establish at the nursing home. We noticed the pride that glowed in the faces of everyone, not because they were on television but because of the strength and joy they felt within themselves for being in positions to help so many others.

WEEKLY MEETINGS

We are always uplifted every time we get a chance to attend one of the Monday-afternoon meetings of the group Mary started. These meetings last an hour and a half. The people begin by holding hands and reminding themselves that their reason for being there is to find peace of mind and to send love to each other. If someone is ill or unable to attend, they always put the thought of that person in the center of the circle.

They begin the meetings by sharing the twelve principles of Attitudinal Healing, as well as the guidelines for group-support meetings, which are used throughout all the Center's groups. These guidelines are as follows:

Guidelines for Attitudinal Healing Groups

1. Our aim is to work on ourselves, to learn forgiveness, and to practice choosing inner peace.
2. In the groups we recognize that love is listening, and we agree to listen with an open heart, to give mutual support, and to practice nonjudgmental listening and sharing.
3. We are here to heal ourselves. We are not here to give advice or to change anyone's beliefs or behavior.
4. We share from our own experience. By risking and exposing our own emotional state, we find common experience that allows for joining.
5. We respect ourselves and each other as unique. We recognize that each person's process is important, not our judgment of it.
6. We support each other's inner guidance. We let other people find their own answers.
7. The roles of student and teacher are interchangeable. They fluctuate from one to the other regardless of age or experience.
8. We practice being present with others, seeing only "the light and not the lampshade."
9. We agree to keep in mind that we always have a choice between peace and conflict, between love and fear.
10. All information shared in the group is confidential.

After reading the guidelines aloud, the facilitator asks who might want to start. The group members share their problems with one another, and of course they immediately find out that they are not alone. Together they form a "cocoon" of unconditional love, doing their best to find other ways of looking at their situations through the application of the principles.

Each member of the group commits herself or himself to confidentiality as well as to not having the goal of changing anyone else. Each commits to not preaching or giving advice but rather to sharing, from a very personal place, where they may have experienced something similar and learned by healing their own attitude.

We are always impressed with how much humor there is as people extend to each other one of the greatest gifts that human beings can give—listening with unconditional love, with no judgments, and with no desire to interrupt the other person. They listen and respond to each other and try to incorporate the principles of Attitudinal Healing into their lives. Rather than feeling attacked in certain painful situations, they are seeing others as fearful and giving a call of help for love.

What has been fascinating is that we have seen depression that had all the earmarks of being chronic completely disappear. We have seen the symptoms of people diagnosed as having pathological senility, problems with memory deficit, and problems in space and time orientation entirely go away.

We are impressed with how many miracles occur when people of any age find a safe environment to be truly helpful and intimate with each other. The power of unconditional love, of creating an environment where you truly feel useful to others, is paramount. These spiritual principles have very practical applications in every part of life and clearly have no age restrictions.

THE HEALING POWER OF FORGIVENESS

We remember well an eighty-six-year-old woman who had a heart condition called angina pectoris. Somehow the medication did not seem to be working and did not bring her much comfort.

One day she was asked if there was anything in her life for which she had not forgiven herself. She thought for a moment and then began to cry. A deep well of tears was released. She said that she couldn't believe what came into her mind in response to this question.

She remembered an incident when she was about six years old when her mother sent her to the corner store for groceries. While there she stole a candy bar when the owner wasn't looking. She had never told a single soul about this incident. She felt so much guilt and shame about it that it had remained her deep, dark secret for eighty years!

Well, what happened of course was that when she finally decided to forgive herself and let go of the past, the medication for her heart condition began to work very well. At last she literally found the comfort she desired. Perhaps we all need someone we trust in this way, to share our inner secrets so that they don't continue to cause us both emotional and physical damage.

John Goodman

The idea of bringing Attitudinal Healing into senior living communities and nursing homes has been gaining wider acceptance and is now being used in several different locations throughout the country. A few years ago John Goodman, managing partner of the Sage Company in Minnesota, not only became familiar with our work but also began offering Attitudinal Healing and other wellness-based classes to his residents.

John's company owns and operates many retirement and nursing homes throughout the country. He is on the cutting edge of helping to create a new consciousness in the services,

care, and communities of older people. When you enter one
of his homes, you immediately feel the heartbeat of the love
that is there in great abundance.

With multiple levels of care and services available to the
residents, many have been involved with John for years. On
a recent visit to Florida, where some of the facilities are
located, we encountered a lively woman in her nineties who
came up to us in the hallway to say hello. We asked her
how she liked living there. She replied that she never had
a son, but if she had, she would have liked him to be like
John. And with that comment she very spontaneously
placed a big kiss on his cheek and gave him a warm, moth-
erly hug. That certainly told us a lot about the lifestyle she
was enjoying at the senior residence.

Very loving hearts and minds continue to create the design
and architecture of John Goodman's retirement communities. There are complexes with schools, cultural community
centers, and even day-care centers, which makes it easy for
younger children, single parents, and older people to inter-
mingle in a way that is both natural and enjoyable for all.
In addition, a multitude of intergenerational activities and
programs does much to make older people feel valued, useful, and alive.

We were asked to give a presentation in Largo, Florida,
where the Sage Company's latest retirement community,
Palms of Largo, recently opened. We gave a public lecture for the community on Attitudinal Healing, and later
that evening we gave a talk to the residents of the retirement complex. Most of them were in their eighties
and nineties.

We were impressed by how responsive this group was in
their willingness to find another way of looking at the world.
They asked great questions, and we had a wonderful dialogue with them. That night we had a group meeting with
the staff about the programs that promote Attitudinal Healing and other forms of self-awareness, which they will continue to implement in their other retirement communities
throughout the country.

You Are Never Too Old to Change

In December 1989 a very powerful teacher came into our lives. She was ninety-three. Her given name was Andrea de Nottbeck, but she liked people to call her Happy. On December 14, 1989, we received a phone call from Geneva, Switzerland, from someone we did not know. The person on the phone later turned out to be the wife of our French publisher. She stated that there was a ninety-three-year-old woman named Happy who had a painting she would like to give to us. She wondered if it would be possible for us to come to Europe the week before Christmas to receive this gift.

Frankly it seemed to us to be a rather strange phone call— it was from a person we had never met, asking us to come to Switzerland right away. We told her the truth, that we were quite involved with Christmas plans and that it would not be possible. We were then asked if we could come between Christmas and New Year's. We said we didn't know but asked her to call us the day after Christmas. After getting more information we would pray on it and make a decision.

We got busy with other things and forgot about this discussion until we received another telephone call on December 26th. We were told that Happy does not speak English, so she could not speak to us. She had a fourteenth-century painting by a Spanish painter that had been in her family for centuries, and she wanted to give it to us. Happy wanted us to have it before she died. Although she was in good health, she wanted us to come right away. When we asked the subject matter of the painting, we were told it was a painting of Jesus Christ.

Curious, we asked why she picked us to have the painting. We were told that Happy had been meditating high in the mountains in Switzerland and when she asked who was to be the caretaker of the painting, what came to her was "*Love Is Letting Go of Fear*—Jampolsky."

We did some meditating ourselves and, to our great surprise, received guidance that we were to go and receive the painting. Two days later we found ourselves in Geneva,

Switzerland, visiting with Happy. She proved to be a remarkable woman, and through an interpreter we were told
some more of the story.

Her husband had died several years before, and they had
no children. Although she had tens of millions of dollars,
Happy said that she had always been an unhappy and bitter
woman. Most people, she said, had found her to be difficult
to get along with. She was frequently provocative and
argumentative.

When she was eighty-five, someone gave her the book
Love Is Letting Go of Fear. She told us it became a daily reader
for her as she continued to read and reread it over the next
year, attempting to integrate the principles into her life by
finding another way of looking at the world.

A dramatic transformation took place in her as she began
to forgive all the people in her life whom she felt had
wronged her. She began to forgive herself for her own mis-
deeds and self-condemnations. She began to have a complete personality change. From a crotchety, angry, and
provocative woman, she became carefree and joyful and
changed her name to Happy. Without our knowing it,
Happy was the one who was responsible for having *Love Is
Letting Go of Fear* printed in the French language years before.

We were shown a French magazine with Happy on the
cover, featuring a story about her inside. The cover photo
showed her flying in a hang glider high over the French
countryside. She was eighty-eight at the time! We heard later
that she went stunt flying in a biplane at the age of ninety-
one. She became a vegetarian and meditated every day. Each
day she had a closer relationship with her Source.

Happy decided that she wanted to give all of her money
to philanthropic organizations, and she had completed this
task by the time we met. The very last material thing she
owned was the painting of Jesus Christ. In her meditations
she heard the inner guidance that although she was quite
healthy, she would be leaving her body very soon, and that
she was to find the next caretaker for the painting.

Happy told us that many people wanted the painting,
including museums, churches, relatives, and friends, and

all had tried to talk her out of giving it to us. Happy said it was very clear that when she was on the mountaintop, she was to give the painting to us to be its caretaker, even though she had never met us.

We spent three wonderful days with Happy. She was one of the most happy, peaceful, detached yet loving people we had ever met. We were fortunate to spend the beginning of the New Year with her also.

On January 2nd, I (Jerry) left for the Middle East because of a previous commitment, and Diane took the painting back to California. We received a phone call three weeks later that Happy had died peacefully in her sleep. She continues to remain a most powerful model for us. Since she was never too old to change, we know that we will never be too old either.

BEING YOUNG AT HEART IS AN ATTITUDE

We continue to learn much from the many older people we meet on our pathway. Those who impress us the most are those who do not seem to pay very much attention to their age. They constantly have the attitude of being young at heart. They are full of zest and enthusiasm for life. They seem to live each day as if they were just born into that day, and that day is a brand-new experience.

These people have taught us that when we look into the mirror, it is more important to focus on seeing smile wrinkles than it is to focus on seeing age wrinkles. They teach us that we need not focus only on the body. Even when their bodies are not feeling so well and they may no longer be able to do the things they once did, they still feel alive, strong, and full of zest for life. The body always remains their friend, not their enemy.

Many of the older people we have visited over the years help keep themselves youthful by continuing to do some kind of physical exercise each day, even when they are confined to a bed or chair. Others continue to exercise outside, walking, hiking, biking, playing tennis or golf.

The older people who seem to be enjoying themselves the most don't seem to dwell on the past or the future. They are peaceful, and it is rare that you see them making judgments about other people. Like young children, they have an enthusiasm for life and all that is in it. One of the secrets of what keeps them alive and enthusiastic about life seems to be that they care about other people, and their hearts are full of love.

One of the principles of Attitudinal Healing that we hear older people quote again and again is that it is important to let go of old grudges or grievances from the past, to not tread heavily. Our many teachers, whom we have had the privilege of visiting throughout the world, have taught us that it really is possible to go forward lightly, with a twinkle in our eyes, with a sense of humor, and with an attitude of forgiveness with every step we take.

We feel that one of the secrets of not getting caught up with myths about the aging process is to stop counting the years or giving your power as a person away just because you have turned sixty, seventy, eighty, or some other supposedly *magical* number. The people who are most active, productive, and happy in their later years seem to be those who do not get attached to myths that tell them that this or that is supposed to happen to our mental and physical capabilities at a certain age or that there is an "appropriate" way to act because of the number of our years.

Part of the secret of aging well is focusing, with full commitment, on finding ways to be helpful to others. This means freeing the curious and silly child that is within you. It means learning to stay in the present—not getting stuck in the past or the future. It is always knowing that there are new opportunities to be useful every day.

In his nineties our dear friend John Fetzer told us, just a few weeks before he died, that every day he looked forward to phoning five people to tell them he loved them. We think that is what kept a smile on his face to his last moment on this earth.

Part of the secret of living fully throughout our lives is keeping our imaginations alive and knowing the powerful blessing that comes our way, regardless of our age, when we practice boundless gratitude every second of our lives.

We are grateful to all of those who have continued to find a way of feeling useful, who count their blessings and not their disappointments, and who have shown us that we don't need to be afraid of the aging process or even death. These people continue to confirm for all of us that life and love are never ending.

Affirmations
1. There is nothing to fear about aging.
2. I am always as young as the innocent and playful child who lives inside me.
3. My mind is always free no matter what is happening to my body.
4. What counts in life is the fullness of my heart and not the number of wrinkles on my face.
5. When I feel useful and helpful to others, I lose my concerns about the aging process.
6. I am never too old to make new choices.
7. I am never too old to learn new things or explore new ideas.
8. I am never too old to make a difference.

❖

CHAPTER FOURTEEN

ATTITUDES TOWARD PEACE

*The ultimate cause
of peace or conflict
is within us,
not outside,
and each of us can
do something about it.*

THE PEACEFUL MIND

If a person is peaceful all the time, regardless of the chaotic and tragic circumstances in his or her life, there is a great tendency to say this person is not responding realistically to life. This person may even be accused of being in denial or of burying his head in the sand like an ostrich.

GIVING OUR POWER AWAY

We live in a society that tends to say that it is not only realistic but healthy to be in a constant state of high tension as a result of all the terrible things that happen in the world. We are taught that it is normal and healthy to be fearful most of the time, that if you are peaceful, you are probably denying the anger you are feeling about being a victim. Many of us grow up with the belief that wars are inevitable and that it is not possible to live in a world where there is consistent peace.

Many of us give our power away, allowing others to determine what to believe or not to believe, what is healthy or not healthy, rather than making our own decisions about these questions. Many people equate being peaceful with being inactive. Part of the purpose of this book has been to underline the possibility that peace has nothing to do with what is happening in our external lives but that it is totally related to what is happening inside us.

The ultimate cause of peace or conflict comes from within us, not from the outside, and we as individuals can all do something about it.

LETTING GO OF THE BLOCKS OF INTERFERENCE

The blocks that interfere with our remembering that our natural state is love and peace include a belief in guilt, blame, fear, revenge, attack, and war. These make up the very core of the ego. Attitudinal Healing is seeing the value of letting go of these blocks so that we can remember that what we are is love and peace, and the recognition that we experience these by demonstrating them in our own lives.

Can we ever really experience inner peace at the same time that we are attacking another person, regardless of the rationale that our egos may offer us? No, we can't. Working for and fighting for peace are two entirely different things. Our fears and ego minds continue to want us to see value in attacking others, hiding from our awareness the fact that by seeing value in attacking, we lose the very peace we are seeking.

Peace is so simple, yet we make it seem so extremely difficult. We need only remember each day that every time we see value in attacking ourselves or another, regardless of the cause, we will lose our peaceful mind.

PEACE: THE ENEMY OF THE EGO

Most of us—and certainly we count ourselves in this—have had a great deal of difficulty experiencing that peaceful state as often as we would like. The reason for this is that our ego thoughts perceive peace as a threat. As difficult as it can be to admit, we each have thought systems within us that look upon peace as an enemy.

Responding to the ego's fears we would do everything possible to destroy our feelings of peace, seeing this as necessary for protecting the ego. So if we are feeling peaceful, all of a sudden, seemingly out of nowhere, there comes a situation in which temptation gets the best of us and we find ourselves judging or condemning. With the speed of lightning and thunder we then find ourselves consumed with attack thoughts and judgments directed toward others or ourselves.

Our egos actually want us to feel fearful and worried about being attacked or deprived. As long as we feel this way the ego is justified. When we are feeling peaceful, it has a radar system that immediately notices our state of peace and is always ready to find a way to put us in conflict.

FIGHTING FOR PEACE

When we attempt to work toward peace by fighting, the very peace that we are seeking becomes as elusive as a slippery fish, because in the process of attacking we are not peaceful. Having attack thoughts in our minds means that we are playing war games with ourselves and others.

We lose our peace of mind by fighting and attacking others, which is only a projection of fighting ourselves. We of course do not want to see this as a projection. Instead we want it to believe wholly in our own perceptions and to believe that the cause of any conflict we are feeling is completely outside ourselves.

Our egos will always choose some form of attack to solve a problem, which can run the gamut from holding judgmental thoughts in our minds to attacking other people physically. On the other hand, our true self, which chooses nonviolence and peace as a way of solving problems, chooses to find love rather than conflict and fear.

THE PEACEFUL MIND

Peace of mind does not have to be dependent on anything in the world we see. It is purely a matter of recognizing our eternal connection with our Source and the love that joins all of life. It is a peace that is only experienced by sharing it with others. You will find that you will not have to say a word to let another person know that you are feeling inner peace. The peaceful vibrations you emit will be obvious to the world and everyone around you.

Many of us have had the experience of hiking in the mountains and coming upon a quiet lake, so pure and still and clear that you could easily see to the bottom. That image can be the symbol of what a peaceful mind is all about.

A peaceful mind is our natural state. A peaceful mind is one that has no confusion and no impurities. A peaceful mind is one that is interwoven with tranquility, stillness, joy, and love.

A peaceful mind has clarity because it does not possess any conflicting attack thoughts, judgments, or fears.

It is in the joining of our peaceful minds and hearts that love extends and expands, reflecting the essence of our spiritual identity.

GIVING PEACE TO OTHERS

Peace begins with each of us. We cannot give peace to others and to the world until we experience it within ourselves. We cannot truly experience that inner peace until we have healed our unfinished business of the past and let go of our grievances, ultimately through forgiveness. Our inner peace is one of the biggest gifts we can give to another and to the world.

To have peace, it is necessary to live our lives with the attitude of peace demonstrated in both our thoughts and our actions. To have peace is to be totally committed, with every part of our being, to the belief that it is possible. Since our thoughts ultimately create our reality, as we think peace, so it will be.

We were both recently inspired by reading a book entitled *Peace Is Every Step*, written by Thich Nhat Hanh, a Vietnamese monk. He states in this book that consciousness can be divided into two parts—the seeds and the manifestations.

Every time a seed manifests itself, it produces new seeds of the same kind. So the more anger we have, the more seeds of anger we manifest and bring into the world. And conversely the more peaceful and joyful the thoughts we have, the more these seeds are multiplied and manifested in the world.

CULTIVATING GARDENS OF PEACE AND LOVE

For several years both of us have felt it helpful to look upon our minds as gardens to be cultivated and nurtured. The garden of love and peace that is in each of us needs constant nurturing. It needs to be watered by our love. Its sun is our appreciation for its beauty and the sharing of this beauty with all others.

At times, if we are forgetful or we fall asleep, weeds of anger, fear, guilt, judgment, and condemnation appear. These weeds serve us not at all. So the moment we notice a weed, we need to pull it out immediately so that love can have the space and the breathing room it needs in order to be experienced.

When we remember to nourish the soil with our forgiveness, we experience our gardens as beautiful, lovely, and majestic, with no weeds at all.

Gardening is one of the pure joys of life, a gift of love and a blessing for ourselves and all others.

The gardener of the soil and the gardener of peace and love are one and the same, pure beauty and love interspersed with purity of peace that is never ending.

AFFIRMATIONS

We can think of no better affirmation to offer than the
thoughts and images of Diane's poem "The Gardener":

> When you wake each morning—
> take all the love I have given you
> and spread it as generously as you can
> on My gardens—
> never stopping to measure.
>
> Your cup will never run empty,
> and I will fill it each night
> at the end of your journey,
> far beyond the limits
> you first thought possible.
> You will nourish the flowers
> and tend the weeds
> and you, My gardener,
> will reap wealth beyond words.

PART III

❖

ATTITUDINAL HEALING— EIGHTEEN WEEKLY LESSONS

*One of the most important questions
we can ask ourselves
each second of every day is,
Will this thought,
will these words,
will this action,
bring about joining
or separation?*

EIGHTEEN WEEKLY LESSONS:
APPLYING ATTITUDINAL HEALING TO
EVERY ASPECT OF OUR LIVES

The following lessons were developed to help retrain our minds to let go of old beliefs and perceptions that keep us in a state of fear and distress. These lessons are aimed at helping us not to be afraid of love and to make all our communications for the purpose of joining, not separation.

There are eighteen weekly lessons. It is suggested that you concentrate on one every week for at least five minutes each morning, as close to awakening as possible and again at the end of the day for five minutes before going to bed. We find it helpful to write the lesson for the week on a card or piece of paper and keep it with you and, if possible, glance at it as many times each day as you find comfortable.

Do your best to be kind and patient with yourself and remind yourself each day that it is only your own thoughts that hurt you.

1. I can choose to see all others either as extending love, or as fearful, giving a call for help.

> *Application:* When others are acting angry, resentful, judgmental, or seem to be attacking me, I always have the choice to see them at that moment as they appear on the surface, or as fearful, giving a call of help for love. When I do not respond in kind, with anger, resentment, judgment, or attack, I can then go inside myself and find my own abundance of love. I can thus choose to respond with love and compassion, not from the viewpoint of their perceived fear.

2. I can choose peace by directing myself to be peaceful inside regardless of what is happening outside.

Application: Whenever I believe that my peace of mind is dependent on what another person does or doesn't do, or on whether or not an event or experience goes my way, I will always be in conflict. It is helpful for me to remember that at any moment, no matter what is going on outside myself, I can actually choose to be peaceful inside. Today I can choose how I am going to feel about myself, others, and the world.

3. Relief from all stress comes from healing the attitudes in my mind.

Application: I can relieve myself of the stress and tension I am feeling right now by remembering that it is not people, circumstances, or events outside myself that are causing me distress. Only my own attitudes, thoughts, and judgments about those things can make me stressful and full of tension.

4. Perception is a mirror, not a fact. As I think, so I see, because angry thoughts project an angry world and peaceful thoughts extend peace to the world.

Application: If I find myself upset today because of what I see in the outside world, I will remember that what I perceive and experience are the result of projecting the thoughts in my own mind outward. All that I see is filtered by the lens of my own past experiences, and this appears outside me. What I perceive out in the world is actually my thoughts made into images, projected outward as if looking into a mirror. As I recognize the reality in this, I can then look back inside myself and see where I am holding on to unforgiving, attacking thoughts about myself or others. As I choose to change the thoughts inside myself, my perception of the world also changes.

5. "I am not a victim of the world I see."[1]

Application: If I am feeling wronged, dumped on, taken advantage of; if I find myself feeling that love is ultimately dangerous and hurtful, I will remind myself at that moment that I am believing that what goes on in the world outside me is the cause of what I think and feel. And I will remind myself that I am not the helpless result of others' thoughts and actions. Since all unloving thoughts about myself project outward and thus determine what I see in the world, I am ultimately a victim of my own thoughts and not of the outside world. When I am feeling unloving or unloved, it is because at a core level I don't believe I deserve to be happy. Today I choose to remember that it is my own unloving thoughts about myself that make me believe that I am a victim; and I can choose to change negative thoughts into loving thoughts at any given time.

6. I will see no value in holding on to guilt and blame by remembering that my attraction to these produces the fear of love.

Application: When I am upset and fearful of love, it is my guilty thoughts about myself and the blame I am placing on others that are keeping me from feeling peaceful and loved. It is not possible to experience inner peace and love as long as I continue to find value in guilt and blame, because these · cannot coexist. Today, as I choose peace through love and forgiveness, all blame and guilt will disappear.

7. "I am never upset for the reason I think."[2]

Application: When I am upset about anything, it appears that what is happening outside me is the cause of my distress. In actuality why I am upset has nothing to do with this; it is instead a reminder, something projected from my own unhealed past. By asking myself the question When, where, and with whom have I experienced this same feeling before? I will quickly uncover the experience from my past that I now need to forgive, heal, and release.

8. "I am determined to see things differently."[3]

Application: There is another way of looking at the world, and today I am determined to find it. Since my perceptions of the world are determined by my own thoughts and my own belief system, and since one reflects the other, I can choose the thoughts I put into my own mind. As I heal my mind through forgiving and releasing my unhealed thoughts and relationships, I will see the world differently. As I choose peace of mind as my single goal and forgiveness as my primary function, my peace and forgiveness will be reflected back in the world I see.

9. Today I choose neither to judge nor to interpret anyone's motives or behavior.

Application: When I feel alone or separate from others, it is usually because I am judging and interpreting their motives and behavior. I often convince myself that I know what's best for another person and that when they do not follow the script I have designed for them, I am in conflict. In recognizing that all my judgments and interpretations about others are perceptions at best, I can give up the illusions I have been holding on to about them, therefore freeing us both.

10. "Health is inner peace, and healing is letting go of fear."[4]

Application: I can be a healthy and healed person, regardless of the form my body has taken. To achieve true health today, I choose peace of mind as my single goal, with all my other efforts and goals becoming *intentions*. In my desire to be completely healed today, I am willing to let go of all fearful and attacking thoughts about others and myself.

11. "Forgiveness offers me everything I want."[5]

Application: When I feel hurt about the hand that life has dealt me, or maybe that another person's actions have caused me to suffer, or when I feel I have not been loved enough, I may find a temptation to hold on to my grievances against others because doing so seems to offer me what I want. Yet, it is this very holding on to grievances that causes my pain, suffering, and conflict. Today I ask myself, What is it I want from life? Do I want happiness? Do I want peace of mind? Do I want to experience joyful and loving relationships? Forgiveness offers me all this and more.

12. Today I will free everyone I see from the bondage of my own judgments by not seeing them through the past pictures I have of them.

Application: As I choose to recognize that the past pictures I have of others are projections of the thoughts, attitudes, and judgments from my own mind, I can release them from the bondage of those projections by giving up my attack thoughts. When I choose to release another person, I am in actuality releasing myself as the warden of my own imprisoning thoughts. As I choose freedom for another, I am choosing also to release myself.

13. "Giving and receiving are the same, and all that I give, I give to myself." [6]

Application: My past experience has often shown me that when I give something away, I won't have it anymore and I will suffer scarcity and loss. It has also shown me that someone has to give to me before I can experience receiving. Today, if I am feeling sad, alone, or lacking in love, I will find someone to cheer up, to offer my companionship to, and to give unconditional love with no expectations of getting something from them in return. By giving what it is I want for myself, I will experience the extension and expansion of love where no one ever loses and everyone gains.

14. Today I will choose to no longer see any value in comparing myself with others.

Application: When I find I am comparing myself to other people, I can now recognize that I am not only being unloving to myself, I am setting the other person up as my enemy. Admiring someone's abilities and aspiring to them as a positive role model is quite different from drawing comparisons and judging oneself or the other person. As I look for and find everyone's own uniqueness and support them in the place where they are, I can also appreciate and enhance myself.

15. Whenever I think I must wait for some time in the future to be happy, I am consciously choosing not to be happy in the present.

Application: Happiness is our natural state of mind. It is a decision and an inner choice. Ultimately it has nothing to do with events or experiences in the external world. When I think that happiness depends on getting something in the future, I will remember that it can only be experienced in the present. Since now is the only moment there is, I can be happy at this time by choosing peace of mind as my only goal and by giving my unconditional love.

16. As long as I believe that anger brings me something I really want, I will be in conflict, and peace will elude me.

Application: Although I know that expressing my anger is a healthy and important part of my human experience, I also know that continuing to hold on to anger has never brought me peace, happiness, or love. If anything, it is quite effective in keeping peace, happiness, and love away. Today I choose to let go of angry thoughts that make either me or someone else feel guilty. I will remember that I cannot experience anger, which is a form of fear, and love at the same time.

17. I can look upon everything I experience today as a positive lesson, without exception.

Application: Many of the negative experiences in the world have no positive aspects in any sense of the word. Yet it is possible to derive some good, some learning, from them so that in the final analysis they can prove in some way to be beneficial. It may be that I learn such lessons as patience, tolerance, compassion, forgiveness, or acceptance. Usually I learn lessons I might never have expected. The belief that every experience, without exception, is a positive lesson from which I can learn generates my willingness to receive the lessons of my experience.

18. As I change my mind, I change my life, reminding me that no matter what the problem, love is the answer.

Application: As I recognize that it is my own thoughts that create the world that I am experiencing, I can choose to change my mind and therefore change what I am experiencing. At any moment I can choose peace over conflict and love over fear. I can become a love giver instead of a love seeker, and a love finder instead of a fault finder. I can teach only love, for that is what I am.[7]

EPILOGUE

What is Attitudinal Healing but a healing and releasing of the past by no longer seeing any value in hanging on to the hurts we once experienced. It is a form of celestial amnesia that results from forgiving others and ourselves.

What is perhaps one of the biggest mistakes that we human beings make? It is giving the power to others to decide whether we are lovable or not.

What is freedom but to have no restrictions in the wonderment and awe felt in the heart of the innocent child that is within each of us, that we experience in the mystery of life?

What is creativity but to honor our Creator, to listen to our intuitive self, to express ourselves beyond the use of words, and to share our love and uniqueness beyond the limits of our own imagination?

What is laughter but the music that comes from taking ourselves lightly as we walk on the pathway to our true home. It is the melody of our true self, whose heart is always smiling. It is a song of joy, knowing with absolute certainty that in our true reality there is no such thing as fear, guilt, and blame.

What is patience but knowing that there is really no such thing as past, present, and future, and that there is only the eternal now in the real world? Patience is natural when we trust and know from deep within ourselves that we are already home and that we need do nothing but share creation's love.

What is intimacy but the willingness to let you "in-to-me-see"? Intimacy is when I am no longer feeling vulnerable or fearful, trusting that if you knew everything there is to know about me, you would still love me. It is the absence of masks, costumes, secrets, shame, and guilt, and it is the willingness to share all of my thoughts with you without the fear of being attacked. It is the dissolving of any barriers between my soul and yours. It is the total expression of unconditional love.

When loving, caring, hugging, and touching become as essential as eating and sleeping in our daily routine, perhaps many illnesses known to humankind will disappear.

When everyone in the world accepts the reality that we are all spiritually joined, there will be no wars, there will be no conflicts, there will be only love, kindness, compassion, growth, and friendship.

What is life but a journey of learning that giving and receiving are the same and that our purpose here is to love, forgive, and to always have a willingness to extend a helping hand to others.

When we have totally released ourselves from the limitations of the past and have only love in our hearts, we can climb beyond the highest cloud and into infinity. With trust and faith our dream of returning to the home we have never really left then becomes our reality. We experience at-one-ment with our Source and each other, in a world where there is only joining and no separation, a never-ending love, and a total absence of fear.

Notes on *A Course in Miracles*

Many of the ideas that we have expressed in this book are based on principles from *A Course in Miracles*, published in three sections: Text, Workbook for Students, and Manual for Teachers. (In the references that follow, we have noted quotes taken either directly or indirectly from the *Course*. The letter T at the end of the quote refers to the Text; the letters W and LES refer to the appropriate section of the Workbook for Students.

Part I
Chapter One
[1]"Health is inner peace..." T-15
[2]"Health is inner peace..." T-15
Chapter Four
[1]"I am never upset for the reason I think." LES-5
Part II
Chapter Seven
[1]"I am not a body..." W-376 and LES-205
Chapter Eleven
[1]"Love is the essence of our being." LES-229
Part III
[1]"I am not a victim of the world I see." LES-31
[2]"I am never upset for the reason I think." LES-5
[3]"I am determined to see things differently." LES-21
[4]"Health is inner peace..." T-15
[5]"Forgiveness offers me everything I want." LES-122
[6]"Giving and receiving are the same, and all that I give, I give to myself." T-222–223
[7]"Teach only love..." LES-195

ABOUT THE AUTHORS

GERALD G. JAMPOLSKY, M.D., and DIANE V. CIRINCIONE are the co-authors of *Change Your Mind, Change Your Life, Love Is the Answer, Wake-up Calls,* and *Me First and the Gimme Gimmes.* They are internationally known lecturers in the fields of business, education, and health. Dr. Jampolsky is the founder of the Center for Attitudinal Healing in Tiburon, California, and the author of the bestselling *Love Is Letting Go of Fear, Teach Only Love,* and *Goodbye to Guilt.* Ms. Cirincione is a private entrepreneur and the author of *Sounds of the Morning Sun.* They are married and reside in Tiburon, California.